LOOKING AT CARRIAGES

By the same author

FUNDAMENTALS OF PRIVATE DRIVING (British Driving
Society)
THE ENCYCLOPAEDIA OF CARRIAGE DRIVING (J. A. Allen & Co.
Ltd.)
BREAKING A HORSE TO HARNESS (J. A. Allen & Co. Ltd.)
DRIVING A HARNESS HORSE (J. A. Allen & Co. Ltd.)
YOUR PROBLEM HORSE (Pelham Books)

LOOKING AT CARRIAGES

SALLIE WALROND

J. A. Allen
LONDON

British Library Cataloguing in Publication Data

Walrond, Sallie
Looking at Carriages. — 2Re. ed.
I. Title
688.6

ISBN 0-85131-552-6

Published in Great Britain in 1992 by
J. A. Allen & Company Ltd.,
1 Lower Grosvenor Place,
London SW1W 0EL.

First published by
Pelham Books Ltd., 1980

Typeset in Hong Kong by Setrite Typesetters Ltd.
Printed in Hong Kong by Dah Hua Printing Co. Ltd.

To Bill

CONTENTS

ILLUSTRATIONS

COLOUR PHOTOGRAPHS

BLACK AND WHITE PHOTOGRAPHS

BREAKS, WAGONETTES AND OMNIBUSES

COACHES, WAGONS AND COACHMAN-DRIVEN VEHICLES

LINE DRAWING

FOREWORD

by HRH The Prince Philip, Duke of Edinburgh

The revival of driving as a hobby and as a competitive sport has naturally created a new interest in carriages. It is difficult enough to get the right sort of horses or ponies but the problem gets worse when it comes to picking a carriage. The trouble is that over the centuries an almost infinite variety of designs, some really beautiful and some interesting, have emerged from the carriage makers' workshops, both for two-wheeled and four-wheeled vehicles. And now, with the introduction of modern technology, the impetus to experiment has started again. A whole new generation of competition carriages is making its appearance incorporating such things as metal-framed bodies, metal poles, disc brakes, shock absorbers and aluminium wheels.

This book has come just at the right moment to help sort out the multitude of names and descriptions of horse-drawn vehicles and their uses.

I rather doubt whether it is possible for anyone to be right in every case about the names of vehicles but it would have to be a very brave man who challenged the author's encyclopaedic knowledge of this subject and I am sure that all enthusiasts will be delighted that Mrs Walrond has compiled this comprehensive and very interesting guide and 'check-list' for horse-drawn carriages.

PREFACE (First Edition)

Attempting to give the correct name to a carriage can create problems for many of the rapidly increasing number of twentieth-century driving enthusiasts.

Vehicles of every conceivable shape and size were built in the eighteenth and nineteenth centuries, to specifications of owners, by coachbuilders throughout the world. Mass production was rarely applied by most of these craftsmen.

Generally speaking, carriages fall into basic categories such as phaetons, gigs, dog carts, breaks, coaches and coachman-driven conveyances.

They frequently took their names from their instigator, as with the Stanhope Phaeton, their builder, as with the Tilbury Gig, their body shape, as with the Roof-Seat Break, the area in which they first appeared, as with the Norfolk Cart, or the purpose for which they were built, as with the Shooting Wagon.

It seems that the naming of carriages did not always follow strict rules and that, where there was a rule, there was usually at least one exception. There are many cases of almost identical vehicles having completely different names. On the other hand there are instances of very dissimilar carriages having the same name.

This book contains a representative cross-section of each main type of carriage.

Sallie Walrond
Suffolk, England

PREFACE (Second Edition)

In assembling this second edition of *Looking at Carriages*, a decade after the first edition was published, I have left the original text and photographs unaltered for historical reasons.

The British Driving Society was formed in 1957 by Mr Sanders Watney and a group of dedicated driving experts who feared that, unless something constructive was done, the art of carriage driving would be lost for ever. These founder members hoped that perhaps 100 enthusiasts might join the Society, but, today, carriage driving is considered, by many people, to be the fastest-growing equestrian sport, and the membership of The British Driving Society has reached about 5,500 and continues to increase. Similarly, both the Carriage Association of America and The American Driving Society are flourishing, as are driving societies in Australia, New Zealand and throughout Europe.

The variety of aspects of this activity has led to substantial, worldwide, demand for vehicles of all shapes and sizes resulting in renewed interest in the art of carriage construction. Many craftsmen are working hard to perfect their skills in all branches of the carriage-building trade; numerous modern techniques and materials are now being used to advantage, and, in some cases, old methods are being rediscovered.

This resurgent interest has created the demand for associated items; harness makers are producing beautiful sets of leather harness made to traditional designs, but they are also making sets from modern manmade materials to withstand the rigour of cross-country competitions. The need for carriage lamps has resulted in some good copies of century-old patterns, and, holly wood is being sought by whip makers to satisfy the requirements of those who want such whips for showing. The skill of horn blowing continues to be practised, and some excellent instruments are being produced, as are the horn cases on the carriages. In addition, sophisticated transport is being specially designed, complete with living accommodation and portable stabling, to cater for a large number of competitors who spend a great part of the summer months away from their homes.

17

The new section of this book is devoted to carriages which have been produced by contemporary builders. It has been written as a guide for enthusiasts who are discovering the pleasure and satisfaction to be had from looking at carriages as we approach the twenty-first century.

Sallie Walrond
Suffolk, England
1991

ACKNOWLEDGMENTS (First Edition)

Compiling a book of this kind is a large undertaking which would not have been possible if it had not been for the kind co-operation of hundreds of people from all over the world.

Curators in museums, carriage collectors and numerous individuals have taken tremendous trouble to provide photographs and information. The author is deeply grateful for their help and support.

She thanks Mr and Mrs Sanders Watney for reading the text and for their invaluable suggestions.

The photographs on pages 33 (top), 151, 154, facing 161 (bottom), facing 177 (bottom), 207, 213 and 226–7 are reproduced by gracious permission of Her Majesty The Queen.

Those on pages 30, 87, 139, 178–9, 201 and 204 are Crown Copyright of the Science Museum, London.

Listed below are just some of the carriage owners, photographers, museums and people who are connected with the vehicles concerned:
Nigel Albright, page 44 (bottom)
Eric Anderson, 47 (top), 56, 84, 85, 93 (bottom), 118, 136, 145
J. de Nerée tot Babberich, 111
W. Bakker, 74, 104, 156, 160, 189 (top)
D. L. Baldwin, facing 80 (bottom), facing 160 (bottom), facing 176 (bottom)
W. Begelhole, 80
Doug Bell, facing 176 (bottom)
Mrs N. Bell, 132, 133
Miss A. Bircham, 45
W. G. Bourne, facing 160 (top), 184
R. A. Bovaird, facing 160 (top), 184
Mrs J. Bradshaw, 87, 204
J. Bradshaw, 96, 192 (bottom), 199 (top)
Breamore House Museum, 181
A. S. E. Browning, 125, 153 (top), 161, 169 (bottom), 170
Mrs G. Brush, 77 (bottom)
Calderdale Museums Service, 215

F. Haydon, 109 (top), 142

Heavy Horse and Driving, 127

Mr and Mrs Colin Henderson, 31, 102, 194

L. Holt, 90 (top), 130

Mr and Mrs John Horton, 47 (bottom), 55

R. Huecking, facing 160 (top), 184

Gregory Hunt, Hunt's Harness, 35, 40, 41 (top), 49, 51 (top), 53, 57, 58, 63 (top), 72, facing 81 (bottom), 134, 211 (top), 214 (bottom)

George Isles, 67, 68, 69, 73, 79, 83, 86, 128 (bottom), 150 (top), 189 (bottom), 205 (top)

Stanley Johnson, 89

Mrs Gladys Kaye, 143 (top), 209, 214 (top)

Transport Museum, City of Kingston-upon-Hull, 96, 192 (bottom), 199 (top)

Mrs L. Lancaster, 126

Mr and Mrs Keith Langan, 59 (bottom)

Museum of Lincolnshire Life, 150 (bottom)

London Transport, 165, 166, facing 176 (top)

Mrs B. McDonald, 51 (bottom), 80

Lt-Col Sir John Miller, KCVO, DSO, MC, 33 (top), 151, 154, facing 161 (bottom), facing 177 (bottom), 207, 213, 226–7

Miss P. F. Millward, 215

George Mossman, 75, facing 80 (top), 95, 99, 110, 113, 135, 137

The National Trust, facing 177 (top)

Norfolk Museums Service, 100–1

Miss F. Lee-Norman, 124

Miss A. Norris, 43

City of Nottingham Arts Department Industrial Museum, 29, 211 (bottom), 217

Gordon Offord, 38 (top), 148–9

Jaoa Castel Branio Pergina, 44 (top), facing 97 (bottom), 177, 219 (top), 222, 223 (bottom)

Mrs G. L. Pethick, 131

D. Pollard, 203

Louis Poltevecque and El Pomar Foundation, Colorado and J. Roblewsky, 146, 167, 188

Kenneth G. Pope, 165, 166, facing 176 (top)

C. Redmond, facing 160 (top), 184

Mrs A. Robertson, 81

Miss R. Rogers, 124

Carreras Rothmans Ltd, 203

Sarah Sandall, 159

Mr and Mrs R. Serjeant, 103

P. Skipworth, 51 (bottom)

Vaughan South, facing 80 (bottom), facing 160 (bottom), facing 176 (bottom)
Museum of Staffordshire Life, 182, 218
Gordon W. Steward, 119
Mrs B. Stewart-Smith, 44 (bottom)
The Museums at Stony Brook, 67, 68, 69, 73, 79, 83, 86, 128 (bottom), 150 (top), 189 (bottom), 205 (top)
C. P. Surcouf, 159
Jay Swallow, 157, 192 (top)
Swiss Transport Museum, 46, 205 (bottom)
S. Thompson, 117
Museum of Versailles, 221, 223 (top)
Mr and Mrs L. Watkinson, facing 96, 119, 126, 190
Jack Watmough, 127
Mr and Mrs S. Watney, 33 (bottom), 54 (top), 109 (bottom), 120, 122 (bottom), 127, 140, 143 (bottom), 158, 181
His Grace the Duke of Westminster, 63 (bottom), facing 81 (top), facing 97 (top)
The Whitethorn Press Ltd, 63 (bottom), facing 81 (top), facing 97 (top)
Ray F. Williams, facing 80 (bottom), facing 160 (bottom), facing 176 (bottom)
Mrs C. M. Wilson, 150 (bottom)
Mr and Mrs R. Winch, 45
Mr and Mrs J. Wort, 146, 167, 188
Postepski Zdzislaw and Teresa Zurawska, 195, 199 (bottom)

The following people have helped the author with her research and with translations. To these, she is indebted: Colin Anson, Countess Benckendorff, Mrs Midge Boag, Mr and Mrs R. Budiselic, Miss J. Cochrane, Mr and Mrs Martin Corke, Senora Farrajota, Miss M. Fowler, Mr and Mrs Donald Graham, Frederick Van Kretschmar, The Rt Hon. Lord and Lady Loch, P. R. Mann, Michael Mart and Bolesaw Taborski,

The author also thanks Miss Anne Grahame Johnstone, for supplying the line drawings of springs, and Mrs Derek Hatley, for deciphering and typing the manuscript.

ACKNOWLEDGMENTS (Second Edition)

Compilation of the additional chapter on modern carriages for this second edition has involved a large number of people. The author is extremely grateful to carriage builders, owners and photographers throughout the world, who have supplied photographs and technical data for this new section. Without their full co-operation, it would not have been possible for this chapter to have been completed.

She thanks Mrs Caroline Burt of J. A. Allen & Co. for suggesting that new material could be included and Mr Elton Hayes, whose idea it was that such material should be based on modern carriages.

The photograph of The Australian State Coach is reproduced by gracious permission of Her Majesty The Queen.

Listed below are some of the many people who are connected with the carriages concerned:

Mr Clive Bampton, page 238, 257 (bottom)
Mr and Mrs Mark Broadbent, 242,(bottom), 248 (bottom), 254, 258
Croford Coachbuilders, 238, 257 (bottom)
Lt. Col. S.V. Gilbart-Denham, 271
Mr Homer Easterwood, 267, 268, 269 (top and bottom)
Mr and Mrs John Gapp, 262
Mrs Eunice Gleissberg, 241
Mr Ian Goodrum, 241
Mr Philip Holder, 235, 270
Mr Ken Jackson, 250
Miss Suzanne Jones, 231
Miss Anne Grahame Johnstone, 240
Mr and Mrs Brian King, 242 (top), 249, 253
Herren Paul and Gustav Kühnle, 255, 259, 261, 266
Mr and Mrs Reg Leftley, 236
Mr and Mrs Michael Mart, 245
Major L. B. F. Marsham M. V. O., 271
Mr and Mrs Rodney Ousbey, 248 (top)
Mr John Parker, 262
Mr and Mrs Keith Randall, 234

Mr Anthony Reynolds, 271
Mr and Mrs Biff Riley, 231
Mr and Mrs A. Russell, 246
Mrs Elizabeth Russell, 235
Mr and Mrs Mick Saunders, 264
Mr and Mrs René Schoop, 255, 259, 261, 266
Mrs Pam Serjeant, 243
Lt. Col. and Mrs Barker-Simson, 236
Miss Susan Townsend, 262
Mr Philip Turner, 246
Mr David Williams, 237, 251, 256, 263, 265
Mr and Mrs Brian Wood and Miss Sarah Louise Wood, 234
Mr Nick Wood, 233, 240, 257 (top), 260

CHOOSING A CARRIAGE

Quoted from Underhill's *Driving for Pleasure*, 1896.

'A good carriage is intended for many years of hard use, not to be thrown aside, like a woman's gown, in obedience to the dictates of any and every whim of so called fashion − and all this goes to show how important it is that the first choice should be carefully made.'

TYPES OF SPRING

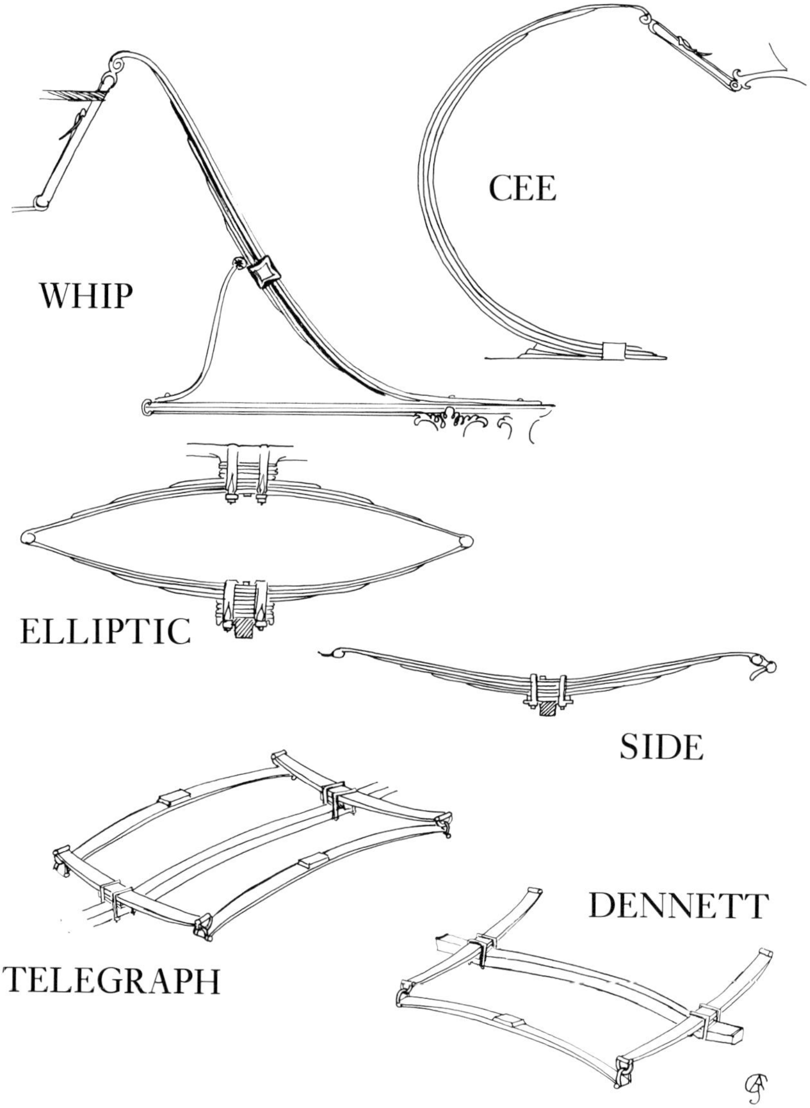

WHIP

CEE

ELLIPTIC

SIDE

TELEGRAPH

DENNETT

Part 1
PHAETONS AND
THEIR RELATIONS

PHAETONS

The name 'phaeton' was first used in 1788. It is believed to have originated from Greek mythology when Phaëthon, who was the son of the sun god, Helios, is reported to have driven his father's chariot. The story is related that the horses galloped off and nearly set fire to the earth before they could be stopped.

Phaetons all have four wheels and were built to a number of designs from the end of the eighteenth century to enable the owner to drive his own horses.

The earliest phaetons were the Crane-Neck and Perch-High varieties, which were also known as Highflyers. These phaetons were said to have 'set all London in an agitation' owing to their remarkable height and extremity of design. It was claimed that the hind wheels of one were eight feet in diameter with the floor of the vehicle set above them. The front wheels were nearly five feet tall. The body consisted of a seat on iron standards, reached by a ladder, from which the Whip attempted to drive his team. The coachbuilder, Adams, is reported to have said that 'to sit on such a seat when the horses were going at much speed would require as much skill as is evinced by a rope dancer at the theatre. None but an extremely robust constitution could stand the violent jolting of such a vehicle over the stones of a paved road.'

The Highflyer was popularized by the fact that the Prince of Wales, later George IV, favoured its use.

A fine example of a Crane-Neck Phaeton can be seen in the Science Museum, London.

Phaetons were built in large numbers throughout the nineteenth century. They came in a variety of shapes and sizes to suit individual needs, being named after their designers, like Stanhope, builders, like Mills, and shape, like Siamese.

SEVENTEENTH-CENTURY PHAETON

This phaeton, which was built in about 1698, is thought to be one of the earliest existing British-made carriages in the country.

The body is supported by two perches. The front wheels have eight spokes and the rear wheels are constructed with twelve.

The vehicle was owned by the Baskerville family of Clyro in Powys, Wales. It is said that from about 1898 to 1923 the carriage was housed in Fullers Coach & Harness Manufacturers' showroom at Bath in Somerset, England, on loan from Dr J. Blake of Manton Grange, Marlborough, who then owned the vehicle. It later went to Nottingham Castle Museum

which was fortunate because Fullers' works were destroyed by incendiary bombs in World War II. The carriage would undoubtedly have perished had it remained there.

Seventeenth-Century Phaeton

The phaeton is at present being restored and will, when work is completed, be on display in the Industrial Museum, Wollaton Park, Nottingham.

CRANE-NECK PHAETON

The Crane-Neck Phaeton is also sometimes referred to as a Highflyer. The name 'Crane Neck' is taken from the shape of the iron perches which were bent to allow the front wheels to turn underneath, giving a full lock. This made it easier to manoeuvre the carriage in narrow streets. They were used in preference to straight pairs of perches which, unless the front wheels were very small, limited the lock of a vehicle to little over a quarter.

When the roads were widened, crane-neck perches went out of fashion. They were considered, by some, to be unsightly and of course they added enormously to the weight of the vehicle.

Crane-Neck Phaeton

The body of the phaeton is hung from whip springs on leather braces at the rear.

The carriage which is illustrated here was built in about 1760. It is lent to the Science Museum, London, by Capt Sir John Lionel Armytage, Yorkshire.

EQUIROTAL PHAETON

The Equirotal (equal-wheeled) Phaeton was patented by the English coachbuilder William Bridges Adams in the 1830s. This inventor disliked the customary practice of having the front wheels of a carriage smaller than the rear wheels. He considered that it was desirable for all four wheels to be of equal size and for all four springs to be level. The problem with front wheels which could not pass under the body of the vehicle was that turning in narrow places was troublesome. This difficulty was overcome by constructing a vehicle which was built in two halves connected by central pivoting bolts, one above the other, between the front and the back, so that it was something like an articulated lorry.

The advantages which were claimed by Adams were considerable. The phaeton could be drawn by a single horse with ease due to the lesser friction from the large front wheels. The driver was always directly behind the horse throughout the turns. The vehicle was said to be perfectly stable in turning. The four horizontal springs of equal height gave a comfortable ride. The noise which was usually experienced in carriages with a wheel plate was absent and this was claimed to make the vehicle suitable 'for persons of delicate nerves'.

Various Equirotal carriages were designed including a Pony Phaeton, Town Chariot, Omnibus and Mail Coach. Working premises were set up by Mr Adams' brother in Drury Lane, London, and by Mr John Buchanan in Glasgow, Scotland.

The idea, however, did not gain favour and little more was heard of Equirotal carriages.

The vehicle illustrated here must be one of the rarest in the world; the author does not know of any other existing Equirotal carriages built on these lines.

The method of achieving articulation between the front and rear portions is different from that described above. In all the previously mentioned designs there were either two bolts, one above the other, or one long bolt at the middle of the vehicle upon which the front and rear parts hinged. This was necessary to hold both parts of the vehicle level. In the carriage illustrated a completely different system is used.

There is a stout beam which can swivel upon vertical bolts

Equirotal Phaeton

immediately above the front axle and rather in front of the rear axle. This beam slides in horizontal slots at the rear of the fore part and at the front of the rear part thus holding both parts level. There is a flat steel connecting rod between the nearside rear of the fore part and offside front of the rear part. This ensures that when the fore part articulates with respect to the beam in one direction the rear part will articulate in the opposite direction.

The main advantages of this system over a central pivot appear to be:
1. When the vehicle articulates in order to negotiate a corner, the outer wheels move apart much more than the inner wheels move together so the vehicle can be designed more closely coupled than it could be with a central pivot.
2. The vehicle can be designed with more elegant lines. With a central pivot, a very long bolt, or two bolts spaced apart, would be necessary to keep both halves of the vehicle level which results in a carriage with a coarse profile at the centre.

This vehicle was built in 1838 by Adams for the Duke of Wellington. It was given to a London museum in the early nineteen-hundreds and was, for many years, in the basement of Lancaster House. It can now be seen in the Carriage House at Dodington Park, Chipping Sodbury, Avon, England.

IVORY-MOUNTED PHAETON

This phaeton, which is probably unique, was built for Queen Victoria in 1842 by Barker and Company and was one of the first cee-spring pair-horsed carriages to be made. All the fittings are ivory and it is a particularly comfortable vehicle. It was renovated in 1961 and is now quite often used at Windsor. It can be driven with two horses, but it was almost certainly designed to be drawn by two or four postillion horses and has been used in this way at some recent shows.

This photograph is reproduced by gracious permission of Her Majesty The Queen.

MAIL PHAETON

The Mail Phaeton, which became fashionable in the 1830s, is one of the largest and heaviest of the phaeton family. It takes its name from the undercarriage which is designed like that of a mail coach, having two sets of telegraph springs, a perch and mail axles. The lock is limited and it was said that it was not a difficult process to overturn the vehicle if a corner was taken too sharply, causing a front wheel to lock against the side of the body.

OPPOSITE:
Above: Ivory-Mounted Phaeton
Below: Mail Phaeton

32

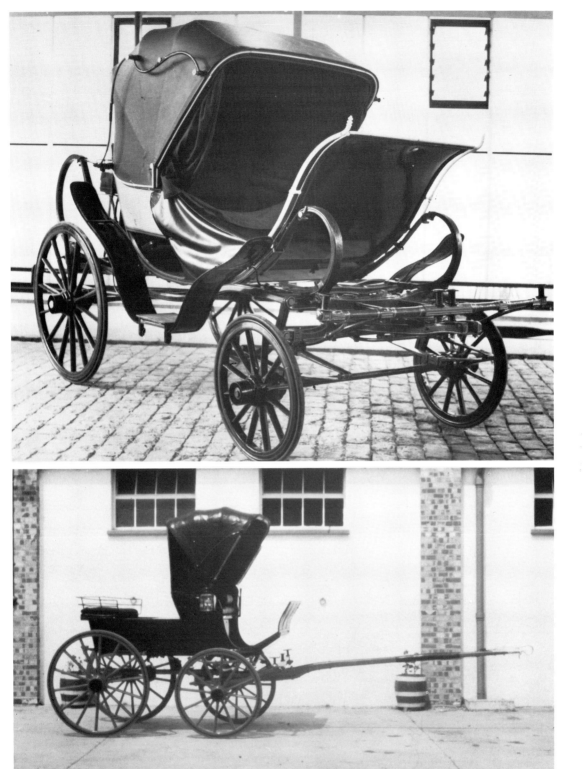

The spacious boot made it suitable for travelling owing to the amount of luggage which could be carried. It was used both in England and on the Continent when post horses and postillions were sometimes employed and was said to have found favour with bachelor gentlemen for long posting journeys in the eighteen-hundreds.

For town or park outings, it was quite usual for a pair of coach horses to be driven by their gentleman owner when a road coach flavour dominated the equipage. Brown collars with black, wheeler harness were quite correct for such a turnout.

At the turn of the century, it was said that the late Earl of Chesterfield turned out one of the finest Mail Phaetons.

Some were designed so that the hooded front seat could be exchanged for the rear, railed seat when the gentleman Whip wished to rest and allow the groom to drive.

The vehicle illustrated here was built by Shanks, the famous London coachbuilders of the nineteenth century. It has been shown by Mr Sanders Watney, driving his coach horses, with considerable success including the championship of all private driving turnouts at the White City, London, in the 1960s.

It forms part of Mr Watney's collection which may be seen at Breamore House near Fordingbridge, in Hampshire, England.

At the end of the eighteen-hundreds a Mail Phaeton would have cost between 100gns and 180gns to buy and £2 2s 0d a year to tax. The weight would have been between 8 and 10 cwt.

DEMI-MAIL PHAETON

The Demi-Mail Phaeton, or Semi-Mail Phaeton as it is sometimes called, is similar in profile to the Mail Phaeton but it has an arch in the body under which the front wheels turn to allow full lock. The undercarriage has no perch, being constructed with either two pairs of elliptic springs or one pair of elliptic and one pair of side springs or a combination of elliptic and telegraph springs. The wheels are usually mounted on Collinge's axles.

This particular vehicle was built by Kimball of Chicago, USA, in 1905, and forms part of Mrs John Friend's collection.

The Stanhope Phaeton is a lighter version of the Semi-Mail Phaeton. It was said to resemble a Stanhope Gig in front with an extension behind on which was put a groom's seat. It was suitable for use with a single horse though when Stanhope Phaetons were used on the Continent they were nearly always driven with a pair.

In England, at the end of the eighteen-hundreds, a Stanhope Phaeton would have cost between 90gns and 150gns to purchase, and 1gn a year to tax providing that it was driven with a single horse. The weight of a Stanhope Phaeton was between 7 and 9 cwt.

The T-Cart Phaeton is an even lighter edition of this branch of the phaeton family. Some people claim that the name T-Cart comes from the fact that a bird's eye view gives the appearance of a 'T'. The front, sticked-back driving seat, accommodates two people. The rear seat is narrower, for just one groom. The vehicle was used with a single horse.

T-Carts were popular at the end of the nineteenth century. It was said that the vehicle was driven by young men of fashion. Their popularity eventually gave way to the Spider Phaeton.

BRISKA PHAETON

The vehicle which is illustrated overleaf was built by Belvalette of Paris, France. It is in Baron Casier's collection in Belgium.

SPIDER PHAETON

(see colour illustration facing page 80)

The Spider Phaeton, which originated in America, is one of the most elegant members of the phaeton tribe.

The body of the vehicle resembles that of a Tilbury Gig. Most have a

Demi-Mail Phaeton

folding hood. The groom's single seat, which is often on branch irons, is connected by an iron framework giving the appearance of lightness. The carriage is usually suspended on two pairs of full elliptic springs.

During the latter part of the nineteenth century it was fashionable for both town and park driving when the gentleman Whip would probably be anxious to show off his magnificent equipage. A pair of highly couraged horses with plenty of action and presence would have been favoured to catch admiring eyes of onlookers.

A Spider Phaeton is suitable for showing a pair of well-bred horses in a private driving class. The fine lines flatter the animals and the lightness allows the horses maximum freedom to show their action to advantage.

Shafts can replace the pole if it is desired to drive a single horse.

A Spider Phaeton is ideal for a concours d'élégance competition when the event is judged from a distance by an artist who chooses, as his winners, the exhibits which he would most like to paint.

The vehicle illustrated forms part of Mr George Mossman's collection in Bedfordshire, England.

SPIDER PHAETON WITH MUD SCRAPERS

A few carriages, such as the one seen here, which is a Spider Phaeton, were fitted with strips of metal to scrape the mud off the wheels as they rotated. This prevented dirt from spraying upwards over the vehicle.

The carriage is in Baron Casier's collection in Belgium.

OFFORD SHOW PHAETON

This elegant phaeton was made at the turn of the century by the famous London firm of Offord, now holder of a Royal Warrant as Coachbuilder to Her Majesty The Queen.

It is suitable for an owner exhibiting a pair of showy horses with plenty of action. The lightness of the vehicle allows freedom of movement. The graceful outline compliments the animals.

There is a rumble seat at the back for the groom, who should wear livery if the vehicle is being turned out to a high standard for a private driving or concours d'élégance class if the occasion is formal.

Lawton, the well-known coachbuilder, also constructed phaetons on similar lines to the vehicle which is illustrated here. These are known as Lawton Show Phaetons.

The photograph overleaf is from Mr Gordon Offord's files in his London office, where he operates as a consultant supervising carriage refurbishing and carriage repairs by contract.

OPPOSITE
Above: Briska Phaeton
Below: Spider Phaeton
with mud scrapers

AMERICAN BASKET PHAETON

American Basket Phaeton with the rear seat folded away

This phaeton, which was made by Van Tassell and Kearney of New York, serves as a dual-purpose vehicle. If the driver wishes to carry a groom, then the rumble seat is left in position. If, however, the owner does not want to take anyone on the rear seat and prefers that the vehicle should appear even lighter than it already looks, then the rumble seat can be folded and packed away under the front seat.

The carriage forms part of Baron Casier's collection in Belgium.

GEORGE IV PHAETON

The George IV Phaeton was originally designed and built in 1824 by William Cook for George IV to enable him to continue the pastime which he had so enjoyed in his younger days when, as Prince of Wales, he drove teams to Highflyer Phaetons. An increase in his weight made it necessary for a lower vehicle to be constructed. This carriage afforded easier access for the Whip. The rumble seat, at the rear, accommodated the groom.

OPPOSITE
Above: Offord Show Phaeton
Below: American Basket Phaeton

39

George IV Phaeton

Gradually, George IV Phaetons became very popular. They were also known as Ladies' Phaetons and Park Phaetons.

During the summer, a Park Phaeton was the fashionable carriage in which a lady could take the air and enjoy driving her pair. The curving dashboard was so designed that it obliterated the horses' quarters from view to save the lady any embarrassment!

A George IV Phaeton is suitable for showing an elegant single or pair in a private driving class. In the USA there are, at some shows, classes especially for George IV Phaetons, when these vehicles are turned out and appointed to an extremely high standard.

The vehicle illustrated here was built in 1909 by Brewster & Co, New York, and forms a part of Mrs John Friend's collection in Wisconsin.

BASKET GEORGE IV PHAETON

OPPOSITE
Above: Basket George IV Phaeton
Below: Canopy-Top Phaeton

This unusual George IV Phaeton is made from basket work. It has a canopy to protect the occupants from the sun.

The vehicle seen here is thought to have been built in Amesbury, Massachusetts, USA in about 1900, and belongs to Mrs John Friend.

CANOPY-TOP PHAETON

The Canopy-Top Phaeton has a removable driving seat at the front. The spacious body is protected by a canopy. There is a box at the back for a small amount of luggage.

This vehicle forms part of Baron Casier's collection in Belgium.

LADIES' BASKET PHAETON

Basket Phaetons were popular for country use. They required less maintenance as there were few painted surfaces.

This vehicle has a wheel cover which is also made of basket work. It was put over the wheel to protect the lady's clothes from mud when she mounted or dismounted.

The carriage can be seen in the Early American Museum, Silver Springs, Florida, USA. It was built in 1900 by Healey & Co of New York.

VIS-A-VIS PONY PHAETON

This English Vis-à-Vis (face-to-face) Pony Phaeton was built in the late eighteen-hundreds as a suitable conveyance for a lady. The low spacious entrance made it convenient for ladies in voluminous dresses.

Ladies' Basket Phaeton

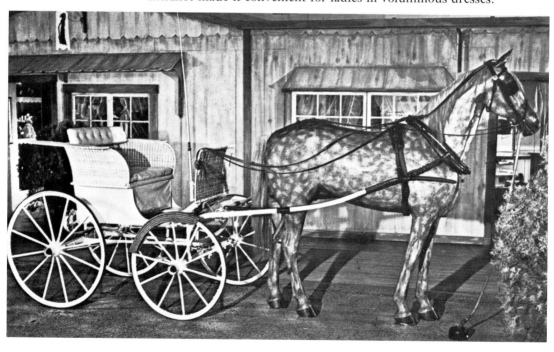

Vis-à-Vis Pony Phaeton

MALTESE KAROZZIN

(*see colour illustration facing page 80*)

This type of vehicle is now used as a conveyance for tourists in Malta and is drawn by mules or horses. There is inside seating for four people who are protected by canvas curtains.

This carriage is owned by Mr Ray Williams and may be seen at El Caballo Blanco, Bodeguero Stud, Wooroloo, Western Australia. It came from the Mount Usher Museum, Dublin, Ireland.

PLEASURE CARRIAGE OF PRINCE CARLOS

The vis-à-vis body is hung on a crane-neck perch undercarriage by cee-springs. The canopy top is decorated with four crowns and trimmed with silver fringes.

The vehicle was given by King Victor Emmanuel of Italy to his grandson Prince Carlos de Bragança (later King Carlos I). It can now be seen in the National Coach Museum at Lisbon in Portugal.

43

Invalid Carriage

PONY CHAISE

The Pony Chaise is a low, country carriage which was designed to accommodate either children or elderly people. The seat is easily reached. The motive power is usually a single pony though sometimes a pair is put to a vehicle of this kind.

The carriage which is seen here was built in about 1890 by Arnold of Lymington, Hampshire, England. It forms part of Mrs B. Stewart-Smith's collection in Surrey.

INVALID CARRIAGE

Numerous invalid carriages were built to enable elderly people to drive in comparative comfort around their estates behind a quiet pony or donkey. The vehicle illustrated here forms part of Mr and Mrs Richard Winch's collection in Norfolk, England.

Wheels of the kind which are seen here, are usually referred to as wire wheels.

OPPOSITE
Above: Pleasure Carriage of Prince Carlos
Below: Pony Chaise

45

MINIATURE CARRIAGE
(see colour illustration facing page 81)

The Miniature Carriage shown is suitable to be drawn by a donkey or small pony, and is said to have been built at the beginning of the nineteenth century. It came from the Duke of Westminster's grandmother's house, Florence Court, County Fermanagh, Northern Ireland, and can now be seen in the Coach House at Eaton Hall Stables, Eaton Hall, Chester, Cheshire, England.

SWISS MOUNTAIN CARRIAGE

This vehicle was built in 1830 and designed to be drawn by a single horse.
   It can be seen in the Swiss Transport Museum in Lucerne, Switzerland.

SWISS RUNABOUT

This Swiss vehicle was built with a substantial perch and hung on transverse semi-elliptic springs. The brake is of the wind-on variety. Draught is by means of a whipple tree.
   The carriage is in Eric Anderson's collection in Belgium.

Swiss Mountain Carriage

Above : Swiss Runabout
Left : Piano Box Buggy

47

PIANO BOX BUGGY

The Piano Box Buggy on page 47 was built at the turn of the century by Septimus Morse of Ballarat, Victoria, Australia. It takes its name from the body shape.

The vehicle has been successfully shown in buggy classes by the Misses Lyndy and Ann Horton and forms part of the family's collection in Western Australia.

DOCTOR'S PHAETON

The Doctor's Phaeton, or Goddard Wagon, is a typical American vehicle giving a quarter lock. The body is hung on transverse elliptic springs onto a perch.

This carriage was built in 1900 by C. A. Stone of Chicago, USA, and forms part of Mrs John Friend's collection in Wisconsin, USA.

JUMP-SEAT PHAETON

The Jump-Seat Phaeton is a Canadian vehicle. It is so named because the small seat behind the dash board can be reversed.

The vehicle is constructed on a central perch and two transverse full elliptic springs. The box-shaped body, which is trimmed with the nickel railings so typical of Canadian vehicles, prevents the wheels from turning at more than a quarter lock. Although vehicles of this type were found to be satisfactory where there was unlimited space they are not ideal for England's narrow lanes when the need to turn sharply can present problems.

The carriage illustrated here was built in 1905 by the McLaughlin Carriage Co Ltd, Oshana, Ontario, Canada, and belongs to Mrs John Friend of Wisconsin, USA.

CUT-UNDER PHAETON

This Cut-Under Phaeton is probably of American origin though it was assembled in England by Mills of Paddington, London.

The body, which seats two people, is hung on two transverse elliptic springs on a central perch. The arch under the seat permits half lock. There is a box behind the seat for carrying luggage and a well under the seat for further stowage. This can only be reached by removing the cushion and lifting the lid.

OPPOSITE
Above: Doctor's Phaeton
Below: Jump-Seat
Phaeton

OPPOSITE
Above: Road Wagon
Below: Whitechapel
Buggy

The wheels are exceptionally fine and made of hickory. They are each secured onto the axle by a single four-sided nut which tightens in the direction of wheel rotation. Therefore, to loosen the nearside nuts the spanner must be applied in a clockwise direction and the reverse for the offside nuts.

This carriage is so light that if it is desired to move it sideways, after the horse has been put to, it can be lifted by the rear axle and positioned as required.

It forms part of the author's collection.

ROAD WAGON

The Road Wagon is another American vehicle with which there is only quarter lock.

This vehicle was built in 1908 and belongs to Mrs John Friend of Wisconsin, USA.

WHITECHAPEL BUGGY

The Whitechapel Buggy is an Australian vehicle which was built around the turn of the century.

The body, which is hung on a perch undercarriage with transverse elliptic springs, permits only a quarter lock.

Cut-Under Phaeton

The seat is upholstered with buttoned leather. The hood is padded and lined with velvet. The dash board is made of patent leather.

The Whitechapel Buggy was generally used as a 'Sunday-best pleasure vehicle' in Australia.

The buggy illustrated on page 51 was made in Ballarat, Victoria, Australia. It has been driven successfully with a pair in three-phase driving trials in Australia by Mrs B. McDonald of Macclesfield, Australia, to whom it belongs.

LADIES' ROAD WAGON

The Ladies' Road Wagon is so named because it is fitted with accessories to make it suitable for a lady's use.

There are looking glasses in the interior. On this particular vehicle, flowers are painted on the body.

This carriage was built in 1900 by Eugene Julien & Cie Ltd of Quebec, Canada, and forms a part of Mrs John Friend's collection.

BUCKBOARD

The Buckboard is an American vehicle, so named because it has no springs and was said to buck over the roughest terrain. The seats are fixed to longitudinal boards which go between the front and rear axles and act as a spring. The Buckboard illustrated here was built in 1906 by G. W. Ogden & Co of Milwaukee, Wisconsin, USA. It has unusual transverse springing at the end of the boards to minimize jarring.

This vehicle forms part of Mrs John Friend's Wisconsin collection.

Many Buckboards were built with just one seat to accommodate two people.

AMERICAN BUGGY

A great many buggies were manufactured by coachbuilders in America. The seat on the shallow box-shaped body accommodated two people.

Suspension was provided by transverse elliptic springs at either end of the perch. The lock was limited to a quarter which could present a problem if the horse turned too sharply.

The vehicle which is illustrated on page 54 forms part of Mr and Mrs Sanders Watney's collection in Breamore House, Hampshire, England.

Vehicles of this kind are frequently referred to as Runabouts.

OPPOSITE
Above: Ladies' Road Wagon
Below: Buckboard

SIDE-BAR WAGON

OPPOSITE
Above : American Buggy
Below : Side-Bar Wagon

This Side-Bar Wagon was made by Mills of London. It was used for showing hackneys. The lightness enabled the animal to move freely with the maximum amount of spectacular action.

The vehicle forms part of Baron Casier's collection in Belgium.

VICEROY

The Viceroy is mainly used for showing hackneys.

The single-seat body is hung on a perch-type undercarriage with transverse elliptic springs allowing nearly half lock.

This vehicle was built in 1978 by Mr John Horton of Western Australia for exhibiting his hackneys.

AMERICAN RUNABOUT

A different type of American Runabout is illustrated overleaf. It is hung on a perch with one transverse and two longitudinal elliptic springs.

The wheels are made of hickory.

The dos-à-dos seating accommodates four people. The tail board lets

Viceroy

55

Above: American
Runabout
Right: American
Runabout (detail)

down on iron supports as a foot-rest for those on the back.

The vehicle has half lock. The front wheels turn under the arch in the body until the tyre contacts the rub iron on the perch which then rotates on its central pin.

The mounting step can be seen and it will be realized that, in order to use this step, the horses must stand to one side so that the shafts and wheels are turned away from the side by which the vehicle is being mounted in order to give room between the front and rear wheels. It is interesting to note that many horses in America, Canada and Australia are so trained that they step to one side to allow the driver to mount and then move across to the other side, without going forward, to permit the passenger to enter the carriage.

This carriage forms part of Eric Anderson's collection in Belgium.

TWO-SEAT CANOPY-TOP SURREY

The Surrey is an American vehicle which was used as a family conveyance. The identical forward-facing seats are fixed to the box-shaped body. Suspension is provided by two transverse full elliptic springs which join the central perch to the buck.

The Canopy-Top Surrey is the vehicle popularly known as 'the Surrey with the fringe on top', as a result of the well-known song from the show 'Oklahoma'.

Two-Seat Canopy-Top Surrey

OPPOSITE
Above: Siamese Phaeton
Below: Buggy

OVERLEAF (PAGES 60–1)
Bugatti Phaeton

This Surrey was built to take either a single or a pair by the Watertown Carriage Company, Watertown, New York. It forms part of Mrs John Friend's collection.

EXTENSION-TOP SURREY

This type of Surrey has a hood which extends to cover the body to protect travellers from the weather. It was designed in North America as a family vehicle and was probably one of the last popular carriages before the age of the motor car. The seating is similar to that of the early automobiles.

The vehicle is in Mrs John Friend's collection and is illustrated here with the top folded down.

SIAMESE PHAETON

The Siamese Phaeton takes its name from its identical forward-facing seats.

This particular vehicle was built by Messrs Mulliner of Birmingham around 1900, and forms part of Mrs Caroline Dale's collection at Darley Dale in Derbyshire, England.

It is an elegant vehicle which is suitable for showing a pair of horses.

Extension-Top Surrey

BUGGY

This is an Australian vehicle which was built at the turn of the century and used as a general-purpose conveyance. It has two seats to accommodate four people but can be converted into a two seater as the rear seat is removable to give a large boot. The body is entered from the nearside as the brake prevents offside entry. It is hung on two long side springs and one transverse full elliptic spring at the rear.

The carriage illustrated originally came from Sydney and now belongs to Mr and Mrs Keith Langan of Armadale, Western Australia. It has been shown successfully in Buggy turnout classes in Australia.

A vehicle of this type is, in Australia, sometimes referred to as a wagonette.

BUGATTI PHAETON

The carriage shown is one of the few to be constructed by Ettore Bugatti. It is built on the lines of a Siamese Phaeton and forms a part of Baron Casier's collection in Belgium.

THREE-SEAT CANOPY-TOP SURREY

(see also colour illustration facing page 81)

The Three-Seat Canopy-Top Surrey is designed to take six travellers. The middle seat is reversible and can be turned to form vis-à-vis accommodation if so desired.

This vehicle was built in about 1905 to take a pair and belongs to Mrs John Friend, USA.

GROSVENOR PHAETON

OPPOSITE
Above: Three-Seat Canopy-Top Surrey
Below: Grosvenor Phaeton

The Grosvenor Phaeton was built by Barker and Company of London to the design of the Grosvenor family.

It can now be seen at Eaton Hall, Chester, Cheshire, the home of the Duke of Westminster, where the Grosvenor family carriages are on view in the Coach House.

Part II
THE FAMILY
OF GIGS

GIGS

All gigs have two wheels and most are built to accommodate two people on a fixed forward-facing seat. If a groom is carried he naturally sits beside the Whip.

Gigs may have descended from the single-seat sedan carts which were used centuries ago. A sedan cart was a sedan chair with a horse for the motive power. The horse was harnessed between shafts which went right down to the axle. There were no springs so the jolting which must have been transmitted from the horse to the traveller would have been considerable. The animal was ridden by the driver who sat with his legs outside the shafts.

Some of the earliest gigs were probably roughly constructed affairs with little more than a board for a seat. This was fixed over the shafts and in some cases hung on leather thoroughbraces to a frame on wheels.

By 1754 a number of two-wheeled vehicles relating to the gig family had emerged.

The Chair-Back Gig made its appearance in 1790. The small, cabriolet-type body was hung on leather braces from whip springs at the back and elbow springs in front. These gigs were sometimes referred to as chaises.

At that time, Rib-Chair Gigs were being constructed. They had a semi-circular shaped board for a seat with ribbed uprights supporting the back rail. The seat design was similar to the present-day Stick-Back Gigs. These early Rib-Chair Gigs were totally devoid of springs. A simple cart like this, which cost less than £12 to purchase and had 'taxed cart' written on the side, was taxed annually at a rate of 12s 0d whilst a more superior version of two-wheeled cart or gig was rated at £3 17s 0d a year.

In 1790, a gig-type vehicle known as a Whisky was also popular.

By the 1830s gigs were mostly suspended on the four-spring Stanhope system. The ash shafts were plated with iron and connected to the axle with span irons which prevented these from having any elasticity. It was said that there was considerable difficulty experienced in keeping the iron stays and plates sound.

Before the coming of the railways, gigs were the most common vehicle to be seen on the roads. They were used extensively by commercial travellers (known then as bagmen) because the boot was large enough to carry samples. They were handy to drive, and park, and cheap to run as they only needed a single horse. In about 1830, several hundred gigs were rented to commercial travellers on an annual basis from one London coach factory alone.

Commuters found gigs ideal for travelling from the suburbs to their London offices each morning and back again in the evening. Every suburban home had its gig house as it now has its garage.

The use of gigs in this capacity was replaced by omnibuses and tram cars.

The introduction of polo was another reason for the upsurge in the demand for gigs. Officers and others drove their polo ponies to matches.

In the latter quarter of the nineteenth century, when gigs were very popular for general use, lancewood shafts were employed to overcome the difficulties which had previously been experienced. They were fixed to the body near the front step and the tapered ends were supported at the rear between two cylinders of India rubber which prevented rattle but allowed a little play. Swingle trees and chain draught to the axle were also adopted.

Gigs were built in a large variety of shapes and sizes. They took their names from their designers, like the Stanhope Gig, or coachbuilder, as with the Tilbury Gig. Some were named from their body shape, like the Round-Backed Gig, or springing, as in the case of the Dennett Gig.

In the late eighteen-hundreds, a gig would have cost between 40gns and 90gns to purchase. The tax payable was 15s 0d a year.

Gigs are now much sought after for use with a single horse or tandem in the show ring. Fortunately there are modern coachbuilders who are producing some fine examples to supply the demand. The cost, new, is in the region of £1,000 for a first-class vehicle of this type.

Italian Gig

ITALIAN GIG

The Italian Gig illustrated on the preceding page was built in Mantua, a province of Lombardy, in Italy, in the seventeenth century.

The seventeen-inch-wide seat is placed well forward from the axle. The wheels are five feet high and have only twelve spokes, which is unusual for a large wheel.

This vehicle can be seen in the Museums at Stony Brook, Long Island, New York, USA. It was a gift, in 1971, from Mr and Mrs Ward Melville and is also known as a Mantua Single Chair.

WHISKY

The Whisky first appeared in about 1790. It is a light, gig-type conveyance which was used for travelling short distances with a single horse.

The name of the vehicle is said to refer to the fact that it 'whisked along'.

The seat of this particular Whisky is hung from the frame by leather thoroughbraces.

Whisky

The vehicle illustrated is thought to have been built in the early nineteenth century.

It can be seen in the Museums at Stony Brook, New York, USA and was
a gift from the Society for the Preservation of New England Antiquities
in 1951.

Boston Chaise

BOSTON CHAISE

The Boston Chaise is a hooded gig which was designed by Chauncey
Thomas and built in America in about 1810.

The body is hung on leather braces.

The vehicle became generally known as a Shay after Oliver Wendell
Holmes' famous poem 'The Wonderful One-Hoss Shay'.

This carriage can be seen in the Museums at Stony Brook, Long
Island, New York, USA. It was a gift of Miss 'Eliz' L. Godwin.

THE WONDERFUL ONE-HOSS SHAY
by
Oliver Wendell Holmes

Have you heard of the wonderful one-hoss shay,
That was built in such a logical way
It ran a hundred years to a day,
And then, of a sudden, it – ah, but stay,
I'll tell you what happened without delay,
Scaring the parson into fits,
Frightening people out of their wits, –
Have you ever heard of that, I say?

Seventeen hundred and fifty-five.
Georgius Secundus was then alive, –
Snuffy old drone from the German hive!
That was the year when Lisbon-town
Saw the earth open and gulp her down,
And Braddock's army was done so brown,
Left without a scalp to its crown.
It was on the terrible Earthquake-day
That the Deacon finished the one-hoss shay.

Now in the building of chaises, I tell you what,
There is always *somewhere* a weakest spot, –
In hub, tyre, felloe, in spring or thill,
In panel, or crossbar, or floor, or sill,
In screw, bolt, thoroughbrace, – lurking still,
Find it somewhere you must and will, –
Above or below, or within or without, –
And that's the reason, beyond a doubt,
That a chaise *breaks down*, but doesn't *wear out*.

But the Deacon swore (as Deacons do,
With an 'I dew vum,' or an 'I tell yeou')
He would build one shay to beat the taown
'N' the keounty 'n' all the kentry raoun';
It should be so built that it *couldn'* break daown:
'Fur,' said the Deacon, ''t's mighty plain
Thut the weakes' place mus' stan' the strain;
'N' the way t' fix it, uz I maintain, is only jest
T' make that place uz strong uz the rest.'

So the Deacon inquired of the village folk
Where he could find the strongest oak,

That couldn't be split nor bent nor broke, –
That was for spokes and floor and sills;
He sent for lancewood to make the thills;
The crossbars were ash, from the straightest t̶
The panels of white-wood, that cuts like chees̶
But lasts like iron for things like these;
The hubs of logs from the 'Settler's ellum,' –
Last of its timber, – they couldn't sell 'em,
Never an axe had seen their chips,
And the wedges flew from between their lips,
Their blunt ends frizzled like celery-tips;
Step and prop-iron, bolt and screw,
Spring, tyre, axle, and linchpin too,
Steel of the finest, bright and blue;
Thoroughbrace bison-skin, thick and wide;
Boot, top, dasher, from tough old hide
Found in the pit when the tanner died.
That was the way he 'put her through.'
'There!' said the Deacon, 'naow she'll dew!'

Do! I tell you, I rather guess
She was a wonder, and nothing less!
Colts grew horses, beards turned grey,
Deacon and deaconess dropped away,
Children and grandchildren – where were they

But there stood the stout old one-hoss shay
As fresh as on Lisbon-earthquake day!

EIGHTEEN HUNDRED; it came and found
The Deacon's masterpiece strong and sound.
Eighteen hundred increased by ten; –
'Hahnsum kerridge' they called it then.
Eighteen hundred and twenty came; –
Running as usual; much the same.
Thirty and forty at last arrive,
And then come fifty, and FIFTY-FIVE.

Little of all we value here
Wakes on the morn of its hundredth year
Without both feeling and looking queer,

In fact, there's nothing that keeps its youth,
So far as I know, but a tree and truth.
(This is a moral that runs at large;
Take it. – You're welcome. – No extra charge.)

FIRST OF NOVEMBER, – the Earthquake-day, –
There are traces of age in the one-hoss shay,
A general flavour of mild decay,
But nothing local, as one may say.
There couldn't be, – for the Deacon's art
Had made it so like in every part
That there wasn't a chance for one to start.

For the wheels were just as strong as the thills,
And the floor was just as strong as the sills,
And the panels just as strong as the floor,
And the whipple-tree neither less nor more,
And the back-crossbar as strong as the fore,
And spring and axle and hub *encore*.

And yet, *as a whole*, it is past a doubt
In another hour it will be *worn out*!

First of November, Fifty-five!
This morning the parson takes a drive.

Now, small boys, get out of the way!
Here comes the wonderful one-hoss shay,
Drawn by a rat-tailed, ewe-necked bay,
'Huddup!' said the parson. – Off went they.
The parson was working his Sunday's text, –
Had got to *fifthly*, and stopped perplexed
At what the – Moses – was coming next.

All at once the horse stood still,
Close by the meet'n'-house on the hill.
First a shiver, and then a thrill,
Then something decidedly like a spill, –
And the parson was sitting upon a rock,
At half-past nine by the meet'n'-house clock, –
Just the hour of the Earthquake shock!

What do you think the parson found,
When he got up and stared around?

The poor old chaise in a heap or mound,
As if it had been to the mill and ground!

You see, of course, if you're not a dunce,
How it went to pieces all at once, –
All at once, and nothing first, –
Just as bubbles do when they burst.

The end of the wonderful one-hoss shay
Logic is logic that is all I say.

STANHOPE GIG

The Stanhope Gig was first built by Tilbury in the early eighteen-hundreds to a design by The Hon. Fitzroy Stanhope. The stick-backed seat, above the large boot, is suspended on two side semi-elliptic springs and two cross semi-elliptic springs. The shafts are plated underneath with iron throughout their entire length and continue in a curve round the rear of the gig.

Stanhope Gigs became popular with bagmen and by about 1830 they were probably one of the most common two-wheeled vehicles to be seen on the road. Numerous improvements gradually occurred such as rubber tyres superseding those of iron. Lancewood shafts replaced the original ash ones, though modern coachbuilders are having to revert to steam bent or laminated ash. The fixed-trace hooks were discarded for a swingle tree.

The vehicle illustrated was built by the famous American carriage builders Brewster & Co, New York, in about 1902, and forms part of Mrs John Friend's collection in Wisconsin, USA.

Numerous modern gigs owe their ancestry to the original Stanhope Gigs.

Gigs genuinely built to the above design are comparatively rare in the United Kingdom, though quite a large number can be found in the USA.

They are suitable for showing a single or tandem in a private driving class.

Stanhope Gig

TILBURY GIG

Tilbury Gig

The Tilbury Gig was originally designed by Tilbury the coachbuilder of South Street, London in about 1820. The stick-back, bootless body was hung on seven springs known as Tilbury springs.

Mr G. N. Hooper, in a paper read before the Institute of British Carriage Manufacturers at York in 1899, gave the following description of it:

> The suspension of Tilburys is really a double suspension, for an under spring is fixed on the axle and attached to the shafts with scroll irons. The Tilbury has a cross spring raised a long way above the hind part of the shaft on a bracket iron: two short elbow springs are secured to the bottom of the curved seat of the body, while two more are attached to the bottom of the body in front. On the proper proportion and adjustment of all these springs depends the comfort of the carriage. If the leather brace which lies at the bottom of each elbow spring is too long, every time the horse's back rises, he causes an action to be set up which exactly resembles the familiar old-fashioned cinder sifter, and which becomes especially disagreeable after a meal.

The shafts and body are plated with metal to give the desired strength which results in a weighty carriage. It was said to be one of the heaviest two-wheeled vehicles to be constructed.

Many Tilbury Gigs were exported, owing to their ability to hold together whilst in use on rough roads.

In 1880, several were on exhibition at the Paris Horse Show. Their wheels were made of hickory which had been imported from America.

In England, the Tilbury had gone out of fashion by about 1850, which is probably why so few are still in existence in Britain.

The Tilbury Gig is also known as the Seven Spring Gig.

This fine example of a Tilbury Gig was built by Brewster & Co, New York, in about 1900, and given to the Museums at Stony Brook, Long Island, New York, USA, by Mrs Alfred B. Maclay in 1952, where it may now be seen.

DUTCH TILBURY

A type of hooded gig which was used in Holland by doctors for visiting their patients. It was also favoured by the farming fraternity for social occasions.

The carriage which is illustrated here was built in about 1900. It belongs to Mr W. Bakker, Insulindelaan 2, Vorden, Netherlands.

Dutch Tilbury

DENNETT GIG

The Dennett Gig was said to have originally been made by a coachbuilder named Bennett and somehow the B became altered to a D. Its name is also attributed to the fact that there were three famous dancing sisters called Dennett on the stage at the time when this gig was first built, and as the vehicle is hung on three springs it seemed appropriate to name it after the girls.

The body shape is similar to that of a Stanhope Gig with a boot under the spindle-backed seat. Two side springs and one cross spring, at the rear, provide the suspension.

The shafts, which are usually made from lancewood if the vehicle is old, or ash if it is modern, run outside the body and end at the rear on each side of the boot.

The gig illustrated here forms part of Mr George Mossman's collection.

Modern carriages of this design are frequently referred to as Spindle-Back or Stick-Back Gigs.

OPPOSITE
Above : French Spider
Gig
Below : English Spider
Gig

SKELETON GIG

The Skeleton Gig closely resembles a Dennett Gig in that it is hung on two side semi-elliptic springs and one cross semi-elliptic spring. The shafts run outside the stick-back seat. The name Skeleton refers to the body because there is no boot under the seat. The dash and splash boards are made of patent leather which is stitched onto a metal frame. The wheels of this particular vehicle are built to fit onto mail axles which are stamped with the name of Selby and the date of 1880.

This vehicle is in the author's collection and has been used extensively for showing both a single and a tandem in private driving classes with great success.

It was found in a hay shed in the mid-1950s and was purchased for £8, delivered home.

FRENCH SPIDER GIG

This Spider Gig was built by Delacouture, Paris, France. The light, spidery body is hung on four springs. At the back there is a metal prop which is used when the vehicle is stored in a carriage house. It enables the gig to be left with its shafts in the air.

This carriage forms part of Baron Casier's collection in Belgium.

Skeleton Gig

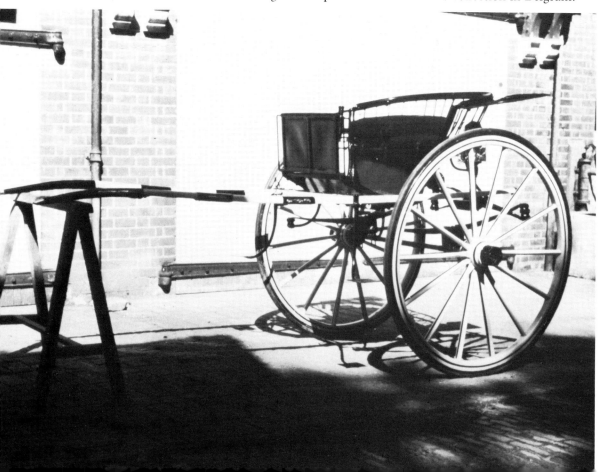

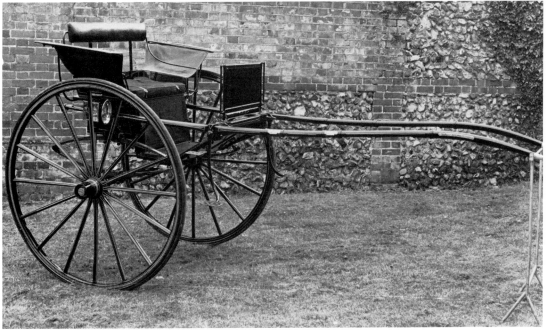

ENGLISH SPIDER GIG

The English Spider Gig which is illustrated on page 77 was built around 1900 by Smart, Moore and Saunders of Reading, Berkshire, and forms part of Mrs Georgina Brush's collection in Essex, England.

TRAY SULKY

This Australian sulky accommodates two people on the adjustable seat and takes its name from the tray-shaped buck.

It is fitted with a hand brake which can also be operated by the right foot against a bar on the lever. The brake lever is held in place by a clip which goes around the lower part of the lever when the brake is not required. The swingle tree is attached to the axle by means of rods instead of chains, which are more usually found with this kind of draught. The body is hung on two semi-elliptic springs. The fronts of the springs are joined to the step irons at right angles.

This sulky belongs to Mrs H. Eames of Western Australia and has been driven with success at major shows by its owner.

Tray Sulky

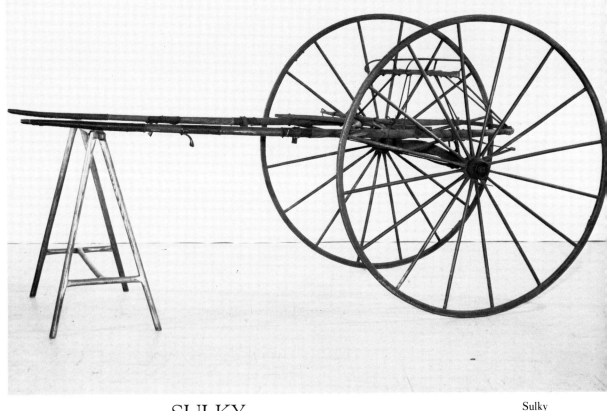

SULKY

Sulky

The Sulky was so named because the single seat permitted the driver to travel alone.

Sulkies were, and still are, used extensively for trotting matches, owing to their lightness.

The sulky illustrated here is known as the Lady Suffolk Sulky as it is said to have been used with the famous Long Island trotter of that name in the middle of the nineteenth century. It can be seen in the Museums at Stony Brook, Long Island, New York, USA.

Modern sulkies are lower and built of metal. The wheels are much smaller than the early editions and they now have pneumatic tyres.

SYDNEY SULKY

The Sydney Sulky is an Australian vehicle so named because the original versions were all made in Sydney. One of the leading manufacturers of Sydney Sulkies was H. H. Stocks of Newton. For this reason these vehicles are sometimes referred to as Stocks' Sulkies.

79

Sydney Sulky

Another well-known builder was F. O'Neill. He varied his sulkies slightly from the Stocks' Sulkies and patented the variations. Many vehicles which are called Stocks' Sulkies were, in fact, made by O'Neill.

In 1908, Sydney Sulkies were shown at an exhibition in Melbourne when they were described as being the most up-to-date examples of the period. It was said that they were the first carriages to have motor-car-type seats. They were often called Motor Back Sulkies. The dash board and body are extensively trimmed with elaborate solid brasswork.

Sydney Sulkies are favoured for use in turnout classes in Australia. The vehicle which is illustrated here has been shown successfully. It has also been used for three-phase driving trials by Mrs B. McDonald of Macclesfield, Victoria, Australia, to whom it belongs.

These carriages are also known as Sydney Brass Show Sulkies.

MALLEE JINKER (SULKY)

OPPOSITE
Above: Spider Phaeton
Below: Maltese Karozzin

The Mallee Jinker was used extensively in Australia in the early nineteen-hundreds. The vehicle takes its name from the area in north-

west Victoria known as the Mallee and was used as a general-purpose conveyance.

The body is hung on two side and one cross spring. There is a leather-covered parcel box at the rear, under the seat, between the shafts.

In order to make it easier for the horse to pull the vehicle through the heavy sand drifts in this part of the country, it was found necessary to fit the Jinker with chain draught. Chains are fixed to the centre of the swingle tree and then fastened at the other end to the axle on each side near the U-bolts which attach the springs to the axle. This method of draught is, in fact, used extensively throughout the whole of Australia and in many other parts of the world.

The vehicle illustrated here forms part of Mrs Anne Robertson's collection in Victoria, Australia. It has been used with great success for three-phase driving events in the 1970s.

This vehicle is referred to as a Jinker in south-eastern Australia and is known as a sulky or gig throughout the rest of the country. It is also sometimes called a Mallee Runner.

SPINNER

The Spinner resembles a gig in many ways. The forward-facing seat is fixed. It is hung on two side semi-elliptic springs. The construction of this vehicle, built by the London coachbuilder Offord in the late

OPPOSITE
Above: Miniature Carriage
Below: Three-Seat Canopy-Top Surrey with seat reversed

Malee Jinker

eighteen-hundreds, is light. The floor is slatted.

The Spinner is ideal for training, exercising a single and 'going for a spin'.

It is possible to drive a tandem from this vehicle but far from ideal owing to the rather low seat which makes it difficult to see the ground beyond the leader.

The low centre of gravity results in a useful cross-country vehicle for combined training competitions.

The Spinner is sometimes referred to as a Speed Cart, Road Cart or Jogging Cart.

The carriage seen here forms part of the author's collection.

AMERICAN ROAD CART

Road Carts were reputed to be originally named by W. S. Frazier and Co, Aurora, Illinois, USA. In 1881 this company claimed that 'the name Road Cart is ours, was first applied by us and distinguishes our form of construction.'

However, the name now loosely applies, in numerous countries, to many types of spinner, jogger or everyday light two-wheeler which can be used for exercising.

Spinner

The vehicle which is illustrated here is said to have been built in about

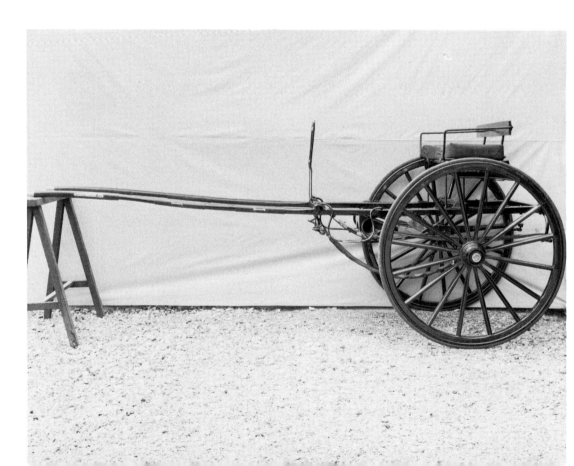

1885. It can be seen at the Museums at Stony Brook, Long Island, USA, and was a gift of Ward Melville in 1971.

BELGIAN ROAD CART

The road cart shown overleaf was built in the early nineteen-hundreds in Belgium. It has an exceptionally wide wheel base. There are steps both at the front and at the rear enabling it to be mounted from either direction. Suspension is provided by just one semi-elliptic cross spring at the back but there are pivoting shackles at the front which permit excellent springing to the body.

The vehicle is in Eric Anderson's collection in Belgium.

BUGATTI ROAD CART

Yet another type of road cart is illustrated on page 85. This particular one was built by E. Bugatti, Paris, France, in 1920. The seat can be moved forwards and backwards along runners by means of a lever, in order to achieve satisfactory balance. The splash boards are made of aluminium. The suspension is provided by three springs. There is a rear prop to enable the cart to be stowed conveniently with the shafts upwards.

The vehicle is in Eric Anderson's collection in Belgium.

American Road Cart

Above: Belgian Road Cart
Right: Rear step on
Belgian Road Cart

Above: Bugatti Road Cart
Below left: Close-up of
Bugatti system of mobile
seat on Bugatti Road Cart
Below right: Lever on
Bugatti Road Cart by
which seat is moved

East Williston Cart

EAST WILLISTON CART

The East Williston Cart originated in Long Island, New York, USA and was a popular vehicle until motor transport took its place. The two seats, which are placed above and between the elliptic springs, are entered from the rear of the vehicle. The seat back folds and the seat is hinged to facilitate entry.

The vehicle here seen forms part of the collection on view in the Museums at Stony Brook, Long Island, New York, USA.

The East Williston Cart is sometimes known as a Meadowbrook Cart.

NORWEGIAN CARRIOLE

This Norwegian gig-type carriage has the seat placed in front of the axle. There is a box at the rear of the vehicle which can be used for luggage. Presumably when this is loaded the contents act as a counterbalance to the travellers, keeping the weight off the horse's back.

The apron at the front is made of leather and designed to protect the driver and passenger from rain and debris thrown up by the horse's hooves.

The carriage was presented to the London Science Museum in 1936 by Edward VIII. It is now in the Museum's store at Swindon, Wiltshire, England, where it can be seen by arrangement.

CEE-SPRING GIG

(see colour illustrations facing page 96)

This gig takes its name from its mode of suspension.

The stick-back body is similar to that of a Stanhope, Dennett or Spindle-Back Gig.

The cee-springs make it an exceptionally comfortable vehicle in which to travel.

The lining, or striping as it is sometimes called, was carried out by Mr E. Burroughes of Botesdale, Diss, Norfolk, England. Lining a vehicle considerably lightens the appearance of the wheels and makes the carriage look more refined.

It would be considered incorrect to add lines of this intricacy to a vehicle such as a Road Coach or Mail Phaeton.

The vehicle which is illustrated belongs to Mr Lesley Watkinson of Halesworth, Suffolk, England.

Norwegian Carriole

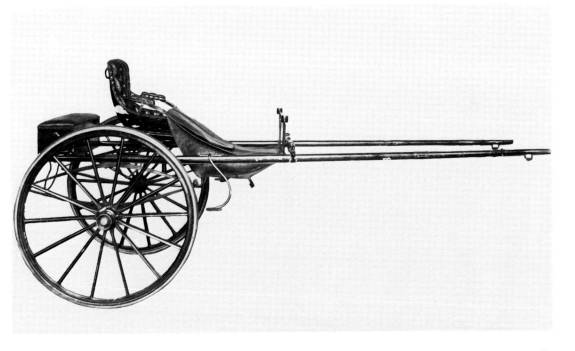

87

ROUND-BACKED GIG

The Round-Backed Gig takes its name from the shape of the solid rounded seat. The body is hung on two side springs and one rear semi-elliptic spring. There is adequate space under the seat for such items as a spares kit, clothing or a picnic, making the vehicle useful for showing and rallies.

This particular gig was built in 1868 by Poad, Helps & Co of Bristol, and belongs to Mrs Jean Cartwright of Leicestershire, England.

CHAIR-BACK GIG

According to Thrupp, the English coachbuilder, in 1877, Chair-Back Gigs of 1790 were hung on whip springs at the rear and elbow springs in front. The body was rounded and had a hood which could be folded. Lancewood shafts ran on each side of the body. The wheels were from 4ft 3ins to 5ft in height.

Modern Chair-Back Gigs, which are now being built by the Harewood Carriage Company, Devon, England, as illustrated here, are entirely different.

Round-Backed Gig

The seat is constructed on a high-tensile steel frame to give an elegant

Chair-Back Gig

line. The body is hung on two full elliptic springs. The laminated ash shafts are joined to the elliptic springs by single leaf springs at the rear. The splash boards are made from laminated ash to give the desired curves.

The weight of the vehicle illustrated is 122 kilos.

BUCKET-SEAT GIG

The Bucket-Seat Gig (shown overleaf) takes its name from the shape of the driver's and passenger's seat.

It belongs to Mr Leonard Holt of Witham, Essex, England.

CUT-UNDER GIG

The Cut-Under Gig was designed and developed by the Harewood Carriage Company in the 1970s, specifically for showing small ponies and donkeys. It had been found that scaling down the Company's larger gigs was not satisfactory as this did not allow sufficient room for adult drivers.

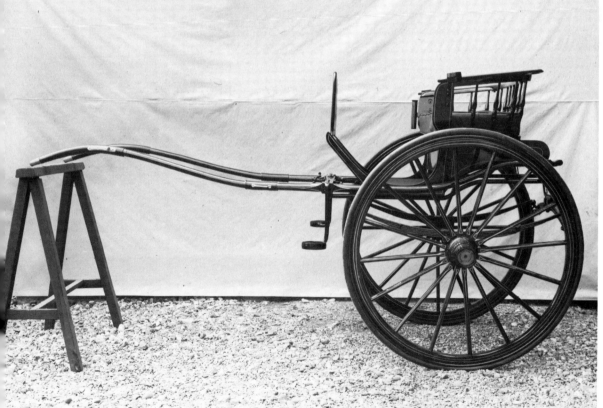

In 1979, the Worshipful Company of Coachmakers and Coach Harness Makers of London, a livery company of the City of London, which was formed over three hundred years ago, decided to present an award annually to the organization which it considered to have made the greatest contribution to the continued use of horse-drawn vehicles. The first consideration would, for a few years, be given to manufacturers. This was awarded to the Harewood Carriage Company of Holsworthy, Devon. The presentation was made at the British Driving Society's Annual Show at Smith's Lawn, Windsor, Berkshire, in June.

The Cut-Under Gig has an ash-framed body with resin-bonded plywood panels. There is a small boot under the stick-backed seat, which is reached by a door behind a valance at the front. The dash and splash boards are framed with metal and covered with padded black butt leather. The shafts, which are made of laminated ash, have matching black leather under the brass tug stops and breeching dees.

The wheels have sixteen oak spokes set into ash felloes. The hubs are fitted with ball races which are said to produce maintenance-free, easy-running axles. The tyres are made of one-inch-solid clincher rubber.

The gig is suspended on one cross and two side semi-elliptic springs made from EN 45A silicon manganese spring steel which is claimed to be superior to the older kind of carbon steel springs.

The gig illustrated here belongs to Mrs Frank Hales of Suffolk, England.

OPPOSITE
Above: Bucket-Seat Gig
Below: Cut-Under Gig

Well-Bottom Gig

WELL-BOTTOM GIG

The Well-Bottom Gig is constructed to enable a small animal to be driven by an adult. The body is shaped to allow adequate leg room so that the Whip can drive in comfort and maintain the correct position. Many such gigs, though not all, have the body hung between elliptic springs on a cranked axle which gives more room for the well-shaped buck.

This vehicle is from the author's collection. It is hung on Dennett springs and has an additional spring at the front, between its lancewood shafts, which results in an extremely comfortable gig.

LIVERPOOL GIG

The Liverpool Gig has a squarer outline than most gigs. There are two seats which cannot be adjusted for balance and the back does not let down as with dog and country carts of a similar profile.

There is plenty of space in the buck for luggage which makes it a useful vehicle for touring and country pursuits. Any difficulty which may be incurred in getting the vehicle to balance correctly can be overcome by placing the luggage in a strategic position. If no luggage is carried then a weight, covered in canvas to protect the paint, serves the same purpose.

A Liverpool Gig is suitable for most present-day driving activities with a single or tandem.

This particular vehicle, which was originally built in 1901, was completely restored by Mr John Gapp of Dereham, Norfolk, England, in 1979.

The cane panels are glued to the sides to lighten the appearance.

POLO GIG

The Polo Gig is said to have been built to enable a polo pony to be driven to the match.

The vehicle was made by Brittain and Sons of Bristol Street, Birmingham, England. It has a hand-operated brake with shoes which act on metal plates on the outer surfaces of the inner sides of the hubs.

There is a basket fitted so that polo sticks can be carried.

The rein rail on the inner side of the dash board is adjustable for height.

It will be noticed that the passenger is permitted the luxury of a padded 'lazy' back to his seat. The driver has a built-up box cushion which puts him into a more comfortable and efficient position from which to control his horse.

The gig is in Eric Anderson's collection in Belgium.

OPPOSITE
Above: Liverpool Gig
Below: Polo Gig
Inset: Close-up of brake on Polo Gig

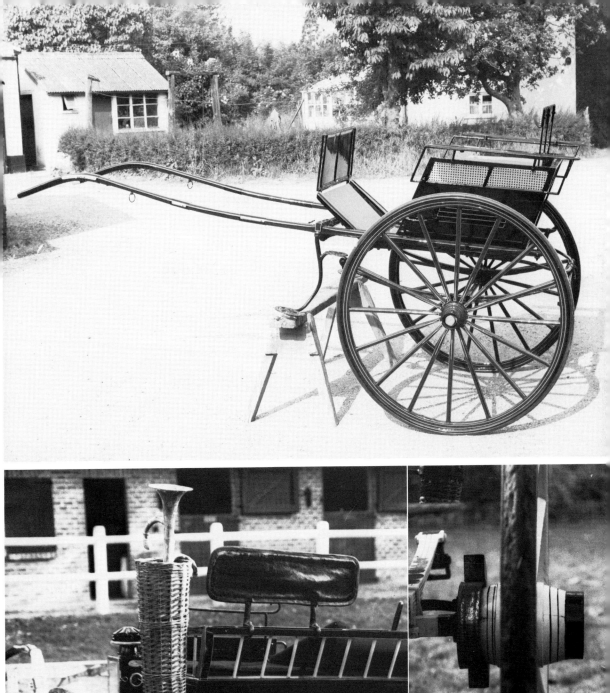

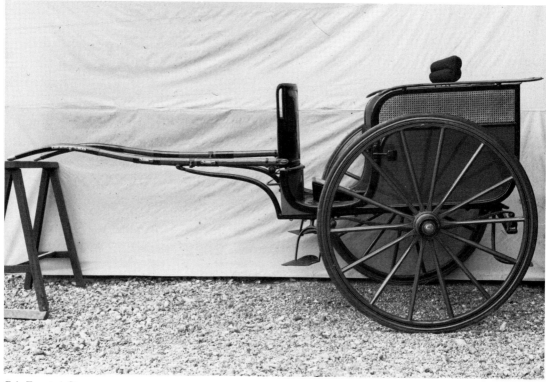

Cab-Fronted Gig

CAB-FRONTED GIG
or MORGAN CART

The Cab-Fronted Gig is so named because the dash board and shafts resemble the front of a Hansom Cab. The patent-leather-covered frame curves to follow the line of the horse's quarters. The shafts, which terminate at the dash, are strengthened underneath by metal and attached to the front of the vehicle by triangular-shaped supports. The body of the gig is built on a metal frame and entered by stirrup steps. These originally had leather toe pieces to prevent the Whip's and passenger's feet from slipping right through the step. The rear of the body lets down to form a useful luggage rack. Hooks are fitted to enable parcels to be safely secured.

The vehicle was built by Morgan, England, towards the end of the nineteenth century. It forms part of the author's collection. When found it had apparently hardly ever been used as the serrated top surface of the steps was still sharp like that of a new stirrup iron. Also, the axles were still of a remarkably tight fit, the closest that the author has ever seen, save in a brand new vehicle.

94

CAB-FRONTED HOODED GIG

(see colour illustration facing page 97)

This Cab-Fronted Hooded Gig was built by Turrell & Sons, 22 Long Acre, London, in about 1880. The hooded body is hung on cee-springs. The ends of the shafts and dash board curve to form an outline which is similar to the front of some Hansom Cabs.

The vehicle can be seen in the Coach House at Eaton Hall, Chester, Cheshire, England.

HOODED GIG

The Hooded Gig supplies the answer to uncertain climates. The disadvantages with the hood up is that side visibility is somewhat restricted.

The curve of the shafts, at the tug stops, enables a larger animal to be driven than if the shafts were straight, without increasing the height of the body of the vehicle. The stirrup steps are another interesting feature of this unusual gig, which is in Mr George Mossman's collection in Bedfordshire, England.

Hooded Gigs are sometimes referred to as buggies.

Hooded Gig

OPPOSITE
Above: Cee-Spring Gig
Below: Cee-spring Gig –
detail of spring

CABRIOLET

The Cabriolet was originally imported from France in the early eighteen-hundreds. It was greatly improved by Count d'Orsay who, with the help of Mr Charles B. Courtney (of Barker & Co, the coachbuilders), lightened the outline and generally made the vehicle more refined. The wheels were raised. The hind ends of the shafts were stiffened and the platform for the tiger (groom) was brought nearer to the body of the vehicle.

Count d'Orsay was very much a leader of fashion where carriages were concerned and his approval of the Cabriolet no doubt contributed greatly towards it becoming accepted as *the* vehicle for 'the man about town'.

In 1840, the Earl of Chesterfield was said to have driven a well-appointed Cabriolet and it is recorded that the Duke of Wellington also regularly used Cabriolets.

The Cabriolet offered plenty of seclusion and protection from the weather. There was a solid leather or wooden apron which fixed across the travellers' legs like a door. The hood gave overhead cover. The head was kept 'half struck' or 'set back' (half open) if it was not required to be closed. This was in order to leave room for the tiger who travelled standing on a platform between the cee-springs, holding onto straps, at the rear of the carriage where his weight acted as a balance.

It was said by Mr G. N. Hooper, in 1899, that the tiger was essentially a London product. The name derived from the striped waistcoats which

Cabriolet

were worn. A tiger was a man in miniature, aged between fifteen and twenty-five years, erect in carriage and immaculate in turnout. The smaller the man, the more he was favoured as he stood in an attitude of defiant perfection below the head of the magnificent horse in his charge. The small figure made the larger equine look even grander. It was claimed that by 1900 the species of tiger was extinct. They were deemed to have disappeared with the Cabriolet just as the mail coachmen and guards became an obsolete race when their particular kind of transport ceased to operate.

OPPOSITE
Above: Cab-Fronted Hooded Gig
Below: Portuguese Cabriolet

The weight and size of a Cabriolet necessitated that a carriage horse of considerable substance and quality should be used. Spectacular action was also desired in order to complete the luxurious picture. If the vehicle was in regular use in London, it was probably necessary to keep two or three such horses which was not a matter for a man with a limited purse.

The Cabriolet was favoured because it could be taken into places where a pair-horse, four-wheeled carriage could not turn. The tiger was cut off from communication except when passengers wished to leave the equipage in his charge. There was almost as much privacy as in a closed carriage and the Cabriolet was said to have been popular for evening use by unmarried gentlemen.

It was usual to hang a bell on the horse's collar to warn other road users of the approach of a fast moving Cabriolet at night.

The Cabriolet illustrated here was built around 1820 and can be seen in the Town Docks Museum, Hull, England.

PORTUGUESE CABRIOLET
(see colour illustration opposite)

This light carriage, which differs considerably from an English Cabriolet, was built between 1767 and 1790 for use by the Portuguese royal family. It was employed mainly by children in the gardens of the royal palaces in Portugal.

The vehicle is lavishly carved and decorated.

It was drawn by a single horse which was driven either from the carriage or controlled by a side postillion.

The vehicle can be seen in the National Coach Museum in Lisbon, Portugal.

CANADIAN CALECHE
(see colour illustration facing page 160)

This Canadian Caleche was built in about 1875. The body is hung on leather braces from cee-shaped irons. It is driven from a seat at the front of the body where there would normally be a dash board. A small dash board is fixed above the splinter bar.

The illustration is reproduced by courtesy of Carling O'Keefe Breweries of Canada Ltd, Toronto, Canada.

CURRICLE

The Curricle, which originated in Italy and was used in France before it was seen in Britain, became extremely fashionable in England in the early nineteenth century, replacing the Highflyer Phaeton as a gentleman's pair-horse carriage. This luxurious equipage was employed both for travelling as well as for town and park driving.

The Curricle is one of the few two-wheeled carriages which was constructed to take a pair. The pole is held up by means of a strap which is passed through a spring under the pole before it is connected to the curricle bar. This, in turn, lies across the tops of the saddles on the horses' backs. It runs through a sideways terret which is fitted to the centre of the substantially padded saddle. The terret is fitted with rollers to allow sideways play if either horse should pull away from, or lean towards, the pole. A bolt at the end of the bar prevents it from being pulled right out of the terret.

The use of the Curricle bar makes it essential that the horses should be of exactly the same height. They must also match for stride and way of going. Ideally they should be of comparable colour. For these reasons, horsing a Curricle was, and still is, an expensive business.

When the groom is seated on the rumble, at the rear, there is no weight on the horses' backs. The vehicle is said to be easy on the motive power.

In the nineteenth century there were numerous reports of accidents concerning Curricles with horses galloping off or falling. The mode of harnessing with a bar made the latter occurrence more likely because if one of a pair went down, inevitably he dragged his partner off his feet too and the Whip would be thrown out as the vehicle tipped forward.

In spite of the disadvantages a Curricle was said, at the time of the Prince Regent, to be 'the most stylish of all conveyances'.

In 1836 both Count D'Orsay and Lord Chesterfield had Curricles built by Messrs Barker.

Lord Petersham turned out a 'brown' Curricle in subtle dedication to a Mrs Brown who featured in his life at the time of the Prince Regent. The harness, horses, vehicle and servants' livery were all brown.

Charles Dickens drove a Curricle as soon as his financial position permitted the luxury.

One beautifully produced Curricle was that which was driven by the first Marquis of Anglesey up to 1854. This is recorded for future

Curricle

generations in a picture by the Hon. Henry Graves.

A vehicle which was said to be 'a nightmare amongst Curricles' was that which belonged to the actor Romeo Coates. The body of the vehicle was made of copper and described as being shaped like a classic sea god's car. Some authorities claimed that it resembled a polished kettle-drum. It was covered with shining brass cocks and shells. The owner's crest, which was a crowing cock, and his motto – 'While I live I'll crow' – apparently decorated every available surface. The harness, on the pair of white horses, was similarly adorned. Romeo Coates' dress was in a dandified vein covered with furs and diamonds wherever possible. When he appeared on stage he liked to be known as 'The Amateur of Fashion' but he was more often referred to, from the pits or the gallery, as 'Old Cock-a-Doodle' or 'Old Turn Coates'.

It seems ironic that the eccentric Coates, famous for his Curricle, should meet his death in connection with carriages. He was crushed between two, in 1848, in London and died at his home afterwards.

Curricles were superseded by Mail Phaetons and Cabriolets owing to the desire for safety.

The Curricle illustrated here forms part of Mr George Mossman's collection in Bedfordshire, England.

Eighteenth-Century
Curricle

EIGHTEENTH-CENTURY CURRICLE

The English Curricle shown on pages 100–1 was owned by the Suffolk family named Kemp. It is unusual in that the body is hung on two pairs of cee-springs and it is without a groom's seat at the rear.

The balance of some early Curricles, in the absence of a groom on a rumble seat, relied on placing a quantity of iron in a box on the hind part of the undercarriage to counteract the weight of the body which was set in front of the axle.

This vehicle is kept by the Castle Museum, Norwich, Norfolk, England, and may be seen by prior arrangement with the Curator. It was given to the Museum in 1904 by Sir Kenneth Kemp, having been owned by his ancestor Sir Robert Kemp who died in 1761. The carriage bears the family coat of arms. Presumably it was built for Sir Robert in the first half of the seventeen-hundreds.

CAPE CART

The Cape Cart is unusual in that it is a two-wheeled vehicle which is designed to take a pair, harnessed in Cape harness on either side of a pole.

The vehicle takes its name from the Cape of Good Hope, South Africa,

Cape Cart

where the cart was first introduced by Dutch settlers.

Queen Alexandra's sons apparently brought a Cape Cart back to England for their mother as a present, when they returned from their world tour in 1881.

The body of that Cape Cart resembled a Whitechapel Cart in many ways, having panelled sides. The rear seat formed a lid for the hind boot and the tail board made a foot-rest. There was a centre seat which could be adjusted enabling six people to be carried. A tilt of white canvas could be hung on wooden hoops to cover the body of the cart.

The Cape Cart which is illustrated here can be seen at Dodington Park, Chipping Sodbury, Avon, England.

It is built to seat two travellers. The body is hung on one cross and two side springs. The pole continues underneath the body of the vehicle to the rear. The traces are attached to swingle trees.

A saddle seat, made of leather, is fitted behind the dash board to enable an African boy to drive.

JOHN WILLIE CAPE CART

John Willie Carts are modern vehicles which are built by the Serjeant family of Burley, Hampshire, England. The Cape Cart enables a pair of ponies, wearing Cape harness, to be driven on either side of a pole to a

John Willie Cape Cart

two-wheeled vehicle. The pole and framework of this carriage are constructed of tubular metal. The body is made of varnished wood.

This Cape Cart easily converts into a single-pony vehicle by removing the pole and putting on a pair of shafts.

It is ideal for exercising and training.

FRIESIAN CHAISE (FRIESE SJEES)

The Chaise which is illustrated here was built in the early eighteen-hundreds, and was originally used in Friesland (a province in the north of Holland) for social visits and for going to church.

The Friesian Chaise was a luxurious carriage employed by both the nobility and farmers. The brightly coloured upholstery was frequently of a velvet type of material or of leather. The body, on many, was lavishly decorated with paintings, gilding and ornate carving. The Chaise was driven from the left side, seating just the Whip and one passenger. It was hung on leather braces between high wheels which were fitted onto a wooden axle.

The Chaise could be driven either with a pair of Friesian horses on either side of a pole or with a single between shafts. If a single horse was put to, the shafts were offset to the off side of the chaise. This was to

Friesian Chaise

Pill Box

enable the horse to keep to the same rut in the road as the off-side wheel, avoiding the rough centre of an unmade track.

This Chaise forms part of Mr W. Bakker's collection in Holland.

The basic paintwork on a Friesian Chaise is invariably white. Harness which has white traces, reins, bridles and trimming is often used to contrast with the black Friesian horses.

PILL BOX

This unusual two-wheeled pair vehicle was built by Dimpre of Paris. It is regularly driven in Belgium by Baron Casier with a pair of horses which are harnessed, on either side of the pole, using a yoke. This is attached near the front end of the pole. Straps are fastened from the base of each horse's collar to either end of the yoke in order to keep the pole in a position which is a little above the horizontal when the vehicle is balanced.

Part III
DOG CARTS AND THEIR OFFSHOOTS

DOG CARTS

Dog carts were built in large numbers throughout the nineteenth century on both two and four wheels to numerous different designs. Generally speaking, they were constructed to enable four sportsmen, out for a day's shooting or coursing, to carry their dogs under the back-to-back seats. The tail board lets down on chains to form a foot-rest for the rear-seat passengers. The sides of the vehicle were built with ventilation slats to make travel more pleasant for the dogs.

From these early dog carts there emerged hundreds of different types of dog carts, Ralli cars, market carts and country carts, taking their names from their designers, builders or places of origin. The varieties of springing ranged from side springs, Dennett springs, elliptic springs, telegraph springs to Morgan and cee-springs. Some had the shafts running inside the body whilst others had their shafts either outside or under the buck.

In England, by the end of the eighteen-hundreds a dog cart could probably be found in almost every coach house connected with a country estate, where it would be employed for such missions as collecting luggage from stations or transporting a businessman to his office as well as for country sporting pursuits.

Four-wheeled dog carts are now generally favoured for pair and team driving both in the show ring and for combined driving events. Good English examples are becoming hard to find.

DOG CART

This Dog Cart, which was built by Mills, would have been used for country pursuits by the sporting fraternity and is now suitable for showing a single or tandem as well as for combined driving events.

This carriage is finished to a high standard. The rear boot is locked by means of a socket-type key. The fittings are covered with small brass discs. The tail board lets down on quadrants. The rear seat has iron side pieces, which hinge upwards as required, when there are passengers, to prevent travellers from slipping sideways off the vehicle.

The carriage forms part of Mrs Jean Cartwright's collection in Leicestershire, England.

ALEXANDRA DOG CART

OPPOSITE
Above: Dog Cart
Below: Alexandra Dog Cart

The Alexandra Dog Cart was built with curving lines. It was thought to be suitable for ladies as the profile was flattering.

Pony Dog Cart

The vehicle illustrated forms part of Mr and Mrs Sanders Watney's collection at Breamore House near Fordingbridge, in Hampshire, England.

The Moray Cart and Battlesden Cart are built on similar lines with back-to-back seating and large sweeping splash boards.

PONY DOG CART

This little dog cart was built to fit a pony and to accommodate four people. The rounded outline is unusual.

The vehicle belongs to Mr George Mossman of Bedfordshire, England.

INDIAN CART OR TONGA

(see colour illustration facing page 160)

This cart seats four people on the inside, back-to-back seats. There are wells both at the front and at the rear of the vehicle for stowing luggage. The seats, side panels and centre back rests are removable enabling the vehicle to be used for both business and pleasure. The interior is decorated with hand-painted pictures, and embossed figurines adorn both the inside and the outside of the cart. The shafts are adjustable for height.

The vehicle forms part of Mr Ray Williams' collection and may be seen at El Caballo Blanco, Bodeguero Stud, Wooroloo, Western Australia.

Tongas were usually less ornate than the one illustrated which was probably a private carriage used by an Indian family. Many Tongas were rather basic constructions, being used as street cabs. They had canvas hoods which were supported on struts coming up from the sides of the body. There were deep pelmets, both at the back and at the front of the hood, to keep the sun from the eyes of the travellers. Some Tongas were fitted with a pole to enable a pair of horses to be harnessed in Cape or Curricle fashion.

HIGH DOG CART

This dog cart is built especially high. The driver's seat is 210cm from the ground which makes it an ideal vehicle from which to drive a tandem (one horse in front of another), or random (three horses, also in front of each other).

The vehicle here seen was built by Offord & Sons of London and is so balanced that it can be left to stand without support. It is in the collection of Mr J. de Nerée tot Babberich of the Netherlands.

High Dog Cart

Tandem Cart

TANDEM CART

The vehicle illustrated here is a copy which Baron Casier made of a Holland and Holland Tandem Cart. It forms part of his collection in Belgium.

The body can be moved forwards and backwards by a lever, on the right-hand side, in order to obtain the correct balance according to the weight of the driver and passengers.

Tandem carts of this type were greatly favoured by the young bloods of the nineteenth century wishing to cut a dash with their tandems and show off to their friends. There are records of various tandem clubs when members assembled to share the thrills of tandem driving with fellow Whips.

1977 saw the beginning of new tandem clubs in America and England, enabling enthusiasts of the two-horse, four-reins brigade to get together. Both clubs are currently flourishing with memberships steadily increasing. Very few members are fortunate enough to own vehicles such as the one seen here. They have to make do with a variety of lower tandem carts, dog carts, Ralli cars and gigs.

COCKING CART

The Cocking Cart was mainly used for tandem driving in the eighteen-hundreds. The high vehicle resembles the front of a coach in many ways, with a boot under the driver's and passenger's seat. Some authorities claim that Cocking Carts were used for taking fighting cocks to the 'main' (cockfight). However, one well-known contemporary Whip says that some bantam cocks which he carried in his Cocking Cart became travel-sick so there is now some doubt regarding this explanation of the origin of the name. It could be that Cocking Carts were used as grandstands at cock fights rather than for the transportation of the birds.

The rear forward-facing seat is built to accommodate the groom from where he is in a position to keep an eye on the progress of his master's tandem and jump down quickly if the need arises.

This vehicle forms part of Mr George Mossman's collection in Bedfordshire, England.

COUNTRY CART
(see also colour illustration facing page 161)

The Country Cart is an offshoot of the dog cart with accommodation for four people on the movable back-to-back seats.

Cocking Cart

Country Cart showing
swingle tree

This vehicle is unusual in that it is fitted with a brake which is not normally found on an English two-wheeled carriage. Harness with a strong breeching is usually adequate for holding back a light two-wheeled cart.

Numerous two-wheeled vehicles of the dog cart and gig type are fitted with a swingle tree and chain draught to the axle. This admirable arrangement is preferable if a breast collar is worn when fixed trace hooks can cause chafing on the animal's shoulders. As the horse goes forward the stride causes the shoulders to move from side to side which results in considerable rubbing if a breast collar is used with solid trace hooks. If an unfit horse is driven for any distance under these conditions he will soon become sore and will quite likely refuse to go forward. Therefore, if a breast collar is used, a swingle tree is preferable. If a swingle tree, also known as whipple tree, whiffle tree, or bar, is used, care should be taken to ensure that it is correctly fitted. It can either be fixed as is shown here by strips of leather which are bolted to the splinter bar, or by straps which are passed round both the splinter bar and swingle tree and held in position by dees, on either, to prevent the straps from slipping sideways. The length of these straps is very important. They must be adjusted so that the draught is on the chains down to the axle. If they are too short the draught may be transferred by them to the splinter bar. If they are too long there is danger of the animal being hit in the hocks by the bar which may result in kicking and an accident.

The vehicle illustrated was the property of the late Mrs Elston of Leicestershire, England.

NORFOLK CART (PANEL-SIDED)

The Norfolk Cart is an offshoot of the dog cart and was first built in Britain's East Anglian county of Norfolk. This vehicle was constructed at the end of the eighteen-hundreds. It accommodates two people on a forward-facing seat which can be adjusted to facilitate the correct balance according to the weight of the Whip and passenger and the location of the luggage which may be carried on the floor.

This carriage is suitable for driving a single or tandem in private driving or combined driving events. It belongs to Mrs J. D. Greene of Suffolk, England.

NORFOLK CART (SLAT-SIDED)

Numerous Norfolk Carts were built with slat sides to allow more ventilation to the contents of the buck. Many were constructed with a

Norfolk Cart (panel-sided)

varnished wood finish which was easier to maintain though, of course, more difficult to build in the first place. Paint would be used to fill and cover irregular surfaces whereas a plain wooden surface required a very high standard before the varnish could be applied. Mahogany and oak were favourite woods for the body.

This vehicle forms part of the author's collection.

OPPOSITE
Above: Norfolk Cart (slat-sided)
Below: Essex Cart

ESSEX CART

The Essex Cart is another country cart which is an offshoot of the dog cart.

The Essex Cart was built with a higher seat than many other country carts making it easier for dealers to see over hedges and into yards. A bargain which might have been missed by a Norfolk Cart driver would perhaps be noticed by those travelling in an Essex Cart.

The 'lazy' back of the seat is formed by a broad strap which can be adjusted as required by means of a large brass buckle.

The straight shafts run under the body. The lamps are set high to prevent the glasses from getting chipped and cracked from stones thrown up from the road.

This vehicle is suitable for tandem driving as well as single harness work.

Stratford Cart

Pony Cart

STRATFORD CART

This Stratford Cart (shown on page 117) was built by Potters, England, at the turn of the century. The body, which has a movable seat for two, is hung on one cross and two side springs. The back does not let down as with country carts of a similar profile. The dash and splash boards are made of patent leather on iron frames. The trace hooks are sprung.

The vehicle belongs to Mr Thompson of Romford, Essex, England.

PONY CART

Pony Carts were built to a variety of designs. This particular edition was constructed by Carpenter of Staines, England. The body, which has a sliding seat, is hung on three semi-elliptic springs and there is a fourth spring between the shafts, at the front, which results in excellent suspension.

The vehicle belongs to Eric Anderson of Belgium.

GYPSY CART

Gypsy Cart

This Gypsy Cart is said to have been built in about 1902 in Cambridge, England. It was acquired by Mr Lesley Watkinson in 1968 by whom it was restored.

The ornate finish is of a type which is favoured by gypsies.

The lining was completed by Mr E. Burroughes of Norfolk, England.

WHITECHAPEL CART

The Whitechapel Cart was frequently employed as a dealer's or bagman's conveyance owing to the amount of room available under the seat for carrying goods. It was also favoured for tandem driving by the sporting fraternity who used it as a shooting vehicle.

The vehicle illustrated overleaf was built by the London Carriage Company and is in Mr and Mrs Sanders Watney's collection at Breamore House near Fordingbridge, Hampshire, England.

Whitechapel Cart

RALLI CAR ON ELLIPTIC SPRINGS

The Ralli Car is a direct descendant of the dog cart. It took its name from a member of the Ashstead Park family called Ralli.

The main distinguishing feature is that the side panels are designed in such a way that they curve over the wheels to form splash boards. Some Ralli Cars were built so that the side panels and splash board were steamed out of one piece of wood to form the desired curve. Others have only a slightly curving side and separate splash boards which are fixed with curved iron braces.

Ralli Cars were built up to and around the turn of the century in comparatively large numbers. The methods of suspension varied considerably.

The vehicle illustrated here is hung between elliptic springs and has the shafts running inside the buck. This carriage forms part of the author's collection.

OPPOSITE
Above: Ralli Car on elliptic springs
Below: Ralli Car on Morgan springs

Ralli Cars are suitable for family driving activities as they can seat four people (two adults and two children) and have adequate space for such items as picnics, a headcollar and spares.

120

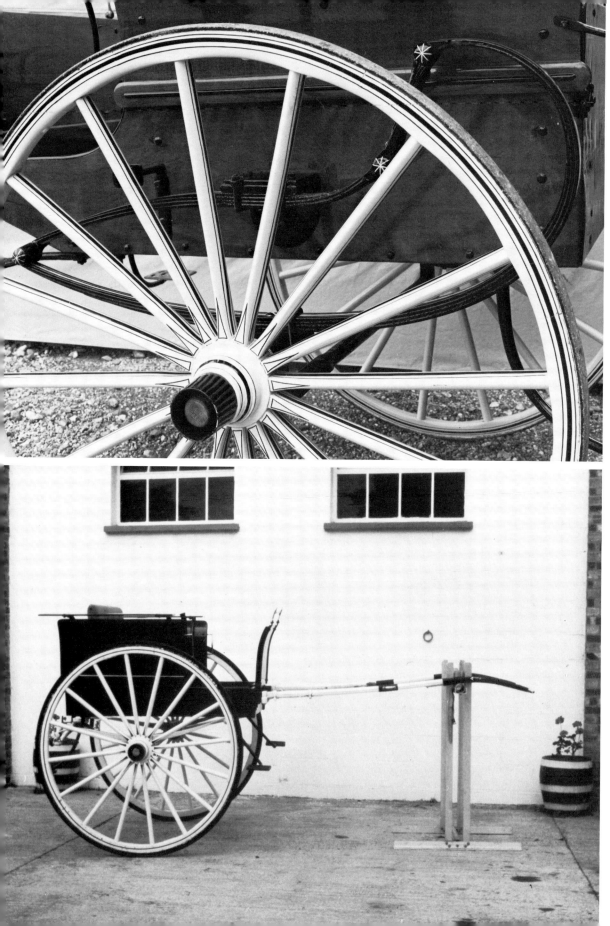

RALLI CAR ON MORGAN SPRINGS

Ralli Car on side springs
with shafts outside

Morgan springing results in a particularly comfortable ride. The vehicle shown also has small springs at the ends of the shafts where they are attached inside the body. This obviates knee rock.

The carriage illustrated here forms part of the author's collection. It was built by Rippon, Yorkshire, at the end of the eighteen-hundreds. The painting of this vehicle was executed by Peter Durrant of Felixstowe, Suffolk, England in the 1970s.

RALLI CAR ON SIDE SPRINGS WITH SHAFTS INSIDE

This vehicle forms part of Mr and Mrs Sanders Watney's collection in Hampshire, England.

OPPOSITE
Above: Close-up of
Morgan spring
Below: Ralli Car on side
springs with shafts inside

RALLI CAR ON SIDE SPRINGS WITH SHAFTS OUTSIDE

This Ralli Car (illustrated on preceding page) has the shafts outside the body. It belongs to Mrs J. D. Greene of Suffolk, England.

JAUNTING CAR WITHOUT CENTRAL SEAT

The Jaunting Car is a traditional Irish two-wheeled vehicle. Passengers sit outwards, facing the sides of the road, on what was sometimes described as 'a dog cart body which was hung sideways'. This seating arrangement was said to put the inexperienced occupant in an extremely insecure position, particularly if the vehicle was driven round a corner at speed. It was also related that, on wet days, keeping the legs and body dry under a mackintosh and rugs was an art which could only be acquired by serving a long apprenticeship.

The Jaunting Car is driven from either one of the side-facing seats or from a forward-facing seat on top of the central luggage well. Sometimes, even if a central seat was fitted, the driver would sit on one side in order to balance the vehicle. The side foot-rests, which (when they are in use) lie

Jaunting Car without central seat

outside the small wheels, are hinged so that they can be turned upwards to make the vehicle narrower for easier coach-house storage. The rear irons enable the vehicle to be stowed with the shafts pointing upwards.

One of the main objections to the Jaunting Car was that of its width, which is excessive. It was said, at the turn of the century, that 'this peculiarity is soon realized'. That presumably meant after a few gate posts and similar protrusions had been accounted for.

Many Jaunting Cars were built with low bodies. This resulted in an excessive slope which was caused by the upward pitch of the shafts. The unfortunate passengers, on such a vehicle, slid either onto their fellow travellers or against the rear seat-rail.

The Jaunting Car is also known as a Side Car, Irish Car and Outside Car.

The vehicle in this illustration is owned and driven by Miss Frances Lee-Norman of County Meath, Eire.

JAUNTING CAR WITH CENTRAL SEAT

Some Jaunting Cars were built with the driver's seat situated over the front of the luggage well. This gives a better driving position in that the Whip is able to face forward and obtain straight purchase with his feet, which helps considerably if the animal 'catches hold'. The disadvantage

Jaunting Car with central seat

of this seat is that there may be difficulty in balancing the vehicle as the driver will render it shaft-heavy, if the weight of the passengers is not sufficient to act as a counterbalance.

The driver of a Jaunting Car was often referred to as a 'jarvey'.

This vehicle can be seen in the Museum of Transport, Glasgow, Scotland, where it was acquired from Templepatrick Riding Stables, Belfast, Northern Ireland in 1964.

DONKEY CART

Flat carts of this kind, which were designed to be drawn by a pony or a donkey, were favoured by costers and totters. They were also used in Ireland for carting churns of milk.

The vehicle illustrated here belongs to Mrs Linda Lancaster of Suffolk, England.

FLOAT

The Float is a low-hung, general-purpose country vehicle.

The body is entered from the back by means of a single step. The seating arrangements vary but very often there is a forward-facing seat on

Donkey Cart

either one or both sides of the rear entrance.

Floats were frequently used for delivering milk. Churns were filled at the farm and the milk was taken to the householders in the area. A ladle, with a hooked handle, was hung on the rim of the churn so that the required quantity of milk could be measured and put into customers' jugs. Some floats had a canopy to keep the sun off the churns.

The vehicle illustrated here is a Pickering Float and forms part of Mr and Mrs Sanders Watney's collection in Hampshire, England.

Floats are now sometimes used for showing horses in light trade turnout classes where the presentation of the equipage is immaculate with great attention being paid to detail. A high-stepping showy animal of hackney or Welsh Cob type is usually favoured.

ICE-CREAM CART

This Ice-Cream Cart was built around 1929 and owned by Penna's Ice Cream.

The words 'Purity' and 'Quality' are written on mirrors on either side of the cart. The windows at the front are trimmed with brass and the top

127

halves, through which the reins pass, are held open by means of a threader handle. The vehicle is said to be difficult to negotiate at blind road junctions as the driver is placed about twelve feet from the pony's head. The noise in the cart is reputed to be considerable.

The cart was being used as a chicken house, with nesting boxes down each side, when it was rescued, in the sixties, by its present owner, Mr Roy Cheeseman of Cottingham, Hull, Yorkshire, England. It is now restored and in great demand for charity functions such as church garden parties.

OPPOSITE
Above: Ice-Cream Cart
Below: Popcorn and Peanut Wagon

POPCORN AND PEANUT WAGON

This Popcorn and Peanut Wagon can be seen in the Museums at Stony Brook, New York.

It was built in 1910 by C. Cretors & Co, Chicago, USA.

BREAD DELIVERY VAN

This English Bread Delivery Van was built in about 1931 by Hovis in their own workshop in Birmingham. It was used for delivering bread in the Hull area for a number of years.

Bread Delivery Van

The vehicle was found and restored by Mr Roy Cheeseman and now forms part of his collection at Cottingham in Hull, Yorkshire, England.

The wheels of the vehicle had to be rebuilt and originally were shod with iron tyres.

BUTCHER'S CART

The Butcher's Cart was used to deliver meat to householders.

The vehicle was constructed in a closed form in order to protect the meat, as much as possible, from flies, dirt and the weather. There is an air vent immediately under the driver's seat. Goods are reached by means of the rear door.

This vehicle forms part of Mr Leonard Holt's collection in Essex, England. It is shown successfully in light trade classes at many of the major shows. Great attention is paid to correct detail of turnout on such occasions. The butcher's apron, for instance, has stripes which run horizontally. A straw boater is worn on the head.

DISABLED DRIVER'S CART

Vehicles of this type were first built in the 1970s to enable physically handicapped adults to have the pleasure of driving donkeys and ponies up

Butcher's Cart

Disabled Driver's Cart

to 12 hands. The shafts bolt into sockets so that the same vehicle can be used for either a pony or a donkey and altered as required. The folding, low-load ramp enables a person who is confined to a wheel chair to be 'run up' and easily secured.

In 1977 the British Driving Society organized a 'Silver Jubilee Drive' when pennants were carried from the tips of England and parts of Ireland, and even from America, to join central points, which finally arrived at Balmoral in October to be presented to Her Majesty The Queen. During this run, money was raised by all the drivers concerned. This was used to purchase suitable vehicles and harness for presentation to the Driving for the Disabled Association.

GOVERNESS CART

Governess Carts were constructed in large numbers around the turn of the century and many were still being built in the early nineteen-hundreds. They were originally designed to enable governesses to take

131

Governess Cart

their young charges for drives in comparative safety. The tub-shaped body is frequently hung between a pair of elliptic springs on a cranked axle which ensures that the centre of gravity is kept as low as possible and the likelihood of turning over is lessened.

The vehicle is entered from a rear door by a low-hung step. This provides safer access for small children than is usually found on two-wheeled vehicles with steps just in front of the wheels. The dangers of being run over if the animal should move forward whilst passengers are mounting and the possibility of getting kicked are eliminated. Once the driver and fellow travellers have mounted, the rear door can be shut. Many have a one-sided door handle which is strategically placed well down on the outer side to forestall children from being able to reach over the door to open it. A door with a double-sided handle can be opened accidentally by being leant against, or on purpose by mischievous infants whilst the governess is coping with the pony. Some rear doors have the handle at the top in the form of a lever. This is easier for the driver to open in a hurry but cannot be released accidentally.

Once the children are inside the vehicle and the door is shut, they are relatively safe in that they are unlikely to fall out as they might do from the high seats of a gig or dog cart.

132

The main disadvantage of the Governess Cart is that it has to be driven from a sideways position at the rear of the right-handed longitudinal seat. Although there is a recess in the seat for the knees, the driver's body has a continual half twist which can become very uncomfortable. It can also be dangerous in that if the horse pulls there is little purchase for the feet to give proper control. Another disadvantage is that if there is need to get to the animal's head in a hurry, great difficulty will be experienced in having to open the door as well as hold the reins, control the horse and put down the whip. Then, having finally got the door open, the Whip has to keep hold of the reins and traverse the length of the vehicle, which may well be moving rapidly by now, before he or she reaches the animal's head. In times of crisis, this could seem like hours.

Some Governess Carts were built to a very high standard by skilled craftsmen. Many beautifully finished vehicles were produced with such refinements as turned wooden spindles along the sides, to lighten the body. Some had brass strips laid into the side panels and edges of the door. Many were produced with a superb varnished wood finish showing the grain of the timber to full advantage. There were, however, numerous Governess Carts which were built by carriage builders with lower standards. Many heavy and rough editions were constructed to supply the demand at the end of the nineteenth century.

Some shows, including the British Driving Society's Show, which is held annually at Smith's Lawn, Windsor, in June, have a class especially for Governess Carts.

Seating and rear door of Governess Cart

It is quite correct to turn out a varnished Governess Cart with a pony wearing brown harness as the whole equipage is essentially 'country'. Painted Governess Carts are more correctly turned out with an animal in black harness. It is, however, quite acceptable to show a varnished vehicle with a horse in black harness.

Seat coverings are frequently made so that they can be reversed, as desired, according to the weather, being of waterproof material on one side and of Melton or similar cloth on the other.

The Governess Cart is also known as the Digby, the Avondale and the Tub Cart. Occasionally it is incorrectly called a Governor's Cart.

The vehicle illustrated was built by Wright of Lowestoft, Suffolk, England, in 1911, and belongs to Mr and Mrs N. Bell of Norfolk, England. The rear-view illustration shows the door and step for mounting. The door handle, which can only be turned from the outer side, is also visible. Note the whip socket placed at the rear to the Whip's right, and also the recess in the seat for the travellers' legs.

BASKET GOVERNESS CART

The Basket Governess Cart obviates the need to maintain painted or varnished surfaces which so easily become scratched or chipped. It is ideal for country use.

Basket Governess Cart

This vehicle forms part of Mrs John Friend's collection in Wisconsin, USA, and was built by the Lawrenceburg Carriage Co, Lawrenceburg, Kentucky, USA, in about 1920.

Princess Cart

PRINCESS CART

The Princess Cart is an offshoot of the Governess Cart. It was designed by Messrs Taylor, coachbuilders of Suffolk, England, in about 1893.

The body shape is similar to that of its ancestor and is hung on the same type of axle and springs. The Princess Cart has the advantage from the Whip's point of view in that it is entered from the front and driven from a movable forward-facing seat at the rear. Passengers are carried, as in the Governess Cart, on inward-facing seats along each side of the body and are able to enter and leave the vehicle without disturbing the Whip.

Princess Carts are comparatively rare.

This vehicle is in Mr George Mossman's collection in Bedfordshire, England.

Above : Demi-Tonneau
Right : Rear view of
Demi-Tonneau

DEMI-TONNEAU

The Demi-Tonneau is said to be one of the most common carts to be found in Belgium. It was used in the early nineteen-hundreds by farmers and would have been driven to market on a week day and to church on a Sunday.

The front seat, to accommodate two people, can be adjusted for balance as it slides forwards or backwards on runners. There is seating for two more passengers at the back who enter by means of a rear door. A low step and substantial mounting handle on the left afford easy access.

The vehicle illustrated forms part of Eric Anderson's collection in Belgium. The rear view shows the door, step, mounting handle and seating accommodation for the back-seat passengers.

FOUR-WHEELED DOG CART

The Four-Wheeled Dog Cart is suitable for driving a pair. A team could be driven if smaller animals were used. If shafts were fitted then it could be employed with a larger single horse.

The high box seat is placed over a slatted boot which was originally designed so that shooting dogs could be carried. It will be noticed that the

Four-Wheeled Dog Cart

front- and rear-seat passengers have separate back rests to give them greater comfort. A small luggage box was sometimes stowed in the space between the backs of the seats. The seats were then placed further apart than is seen here.

Full lock is permitted by the design of the body and four elliptic springs.

The tail board lets down to form a foot-rest. It is held in position by two short chains.

This fine English example is in Mr George Mossman's collection at Luton, Bedfordshire, England.

CONTINENTAL DOG CART

This particular Continental Dog Cart has a rather angular profile.

If only two people are travelling, the rear seat can be hinged up against the back of the front seat to act as a draught excluder. It is held in this position by a strap which fits over a stud.

The felloes of this dog cart's wheels are unusual in that they are made entirely of iron. The spoke ends fit into round cases resembling small egg cups.

The carriage is in the author's collection.

Continental Dog Cart

Eridge Cart

ERIDGE CART

The Eridge Cart is a type of phaeton which is thought to have been designed by Lord Abergavenny. The vehicle illustrated here is in the possession of the Science Museum, London, and is said to have come from Eridge Castle on the Kentish Abergavenny Estate in England.

The seating arrangement is similar to that of a dog cart, being back to back, to accommodate four people.

Low access and a full lock make this carriage very convenient.

FOUR-WHEELED RALLI CAR

The Four-Wheeled Ralli Car is another offshoot of the dog cart, with a similar dos-à-dos seating arrangement for four people. There is room under the seat for luggage.

This vehicle can be used either with shafts for a single horse or with a pole for a pair, unicorn or team. It is suitable for showing in private

Four-Wheeled Ralli Car   driving classes and for use in combined driving trials.
This Ralli Car forms part of Mr and Mrs Sanders Watney's collection.

Part IV

BREAKS, WAGONETTES AND OMNIBUSES

Sporting Break

SPORTING BREAK

The Break is an open four-wheeled vehicle which was used from the mid-nineteenth century by gentlemen for country pursuits.

Breaks varied in shape and were built to satisfy individual requirements. Many were constructed to seat six travellers and had adequate boot space for guns, dogs and game.

The break illustrated here seats eight people. It was built by Whitlock.

SKELETON BREAK

The Skeleton Break was used for breaking young horses.

An old horse, who could be relied upon to stand his ground and remain unperturbed under all circumstances, would be placed on one side of the pole. A youngster would be harnessed on the other side and held firmly by the schoolmaster. The trainer was seated well above the youngster from where he was in a good position to control the newcomer.

The break consisted of a heavy perch undercarriage and four wheels

OPPOSITE
Above: Skeleton Break
Below: Exercising Break

142

Break

which were set well apart. There was a platform behind the seat on which the groom travelled. The pole, splinter bar and dash board were often heavily padded with leather to give more protection.

Skeleton Breaks were kept by most large companies where numbers of horses were being broken. They were sometimes referred to as Dealers' Breaks.

The vehicle illustrated was built by Holmes of Derby and London, England, and formed part of the late Robert Kaye's collection.

EXERCISING BREAK

This Exercising Break (shown on preceding page) is suitable, as the name suggests, for exercising a team of coach horses.

BREAK

This particular break was constructed on a substantial undercarriage making it suitable for rugged work. It has a perch and telegraph springs. The wheels are on mail axles.

The break forms part of Baron Casier's collection in Belgium.

Above : Stable Break with
rear seat reversed
Left : Stable Break
showing front seat hinged

145

STABLE BREAK

The Stable Break accommodates four people. It is designed to be entered from the left only, having mounting steps on the near side. When the seats are in the forward-facing position, the rear accommodation is reached by the front of the vehicle. The nearside front seat hinges sideways to permit rear passengers to mount. They are then trapped in the back of the vehicle by the front-seat travellers. The rear seating can be reversed so that it resembles that of a four-wheeled dog cart. The rear passengers then face the back. The tail board lets down to form a foot-rest and the seats are reached by a rear step.

The rear-view illustration shows the rear lamp situated on the nearside for continental driving. English carriages carry their rear light on the offside.

The vehicle forms part of Eric Anderson's collection in Belgium.

AMERICAN BREAK

This break was built by Frandau of New York City, USA.

It was used as fast coach transporation from Colorado Springs to Denver, Colorado, which is about seventy miles. It used to leave

American Break

Colorado Springs at 10 am and arrive at Denver eight hours later, changing horses four times.

The carriage was purchased from Chester A. Arthur in 1936 by Spencer Penrose who was one of the co-founders of the Broadmoor Hotel, Colorado Springs.

The vehicle can be seen in El Pomar Carriage House Museum, Colorado, USA.

SHOOTING BREAK

The Shooting Break illustrated on pages 148–9 was built in the early nineteen-hundreds by the famous London firm, Peters, who were reputed to be one of the finest coachbuilders in England.

The vehicle would have been ideal for shooting parties as it accommodated six people and had plenty of room for dogs under the rear seats.

The body is hung on two pairs of elliptic springs.

The photograph comes from Mr Gordon Offord's files at his London office.

HUNTING WAGON

The Hunting Wagon is also known as a Park or Commissionary Wagon.

The vehicle illustrated on page 150 was built by Henry Hooker & Co, New Haven, Connecticut, USA, in about 1910. It can be seen in the Museums at Stony Brook, Long Island, New York, USA.

CARRIER'S CART

The Carrier's Cart illustrated on page 150 was built by Hayes and Son of Stamford, Lincolnshire, England, in 1897. There is folding seating for twelve as well as the driver.

The vehicle is finished in bottle green and lined in white. It has a black canvas tilt.

The cart was used for some time on the Earl of Ancaster's estate at Normanton in Rutland. Then, after 1914, it was transferred to the Earl's Grimsthorpe estate near Bourne in Lincolnshire, where it was used as a luncheon van for shooting parties. On occasions such as these, the cavalcade of vehicles which made its way from Grimsthorpe Castle to the shooting marquee included the Carrier's Cart, a Cartridge Cart, two Game Carts, and various conveyances for the servants.

The Carrier's Cart was also used as market garden transport.

This vehicle can be seen in the Museum of Lincolnshire Life, Burton Road, Lincoln, England.

OVERLEAF
Shooting Break

Sandringham Game Cart

Right: Hunting Wagon
Below: Carrier's Cart

SANDRINGHAM GAME CART

The Game Cart shown on the preceding page was used for many years on the Sandringham Estate in Norfolk, England, probably drawn by two Suffolk Punch or Shire horses and designed to carry about 250 brace of pheasants or other game birds.

CHAR-A-BANC

The Char-à-Banc (car with benches) first appeared in England in the early 1840s when one, which was suitable for a team, was presented to Queen Victoria by King Louis Philippe of France. This vehicle had four forward-facing seats, each holding three people.

The Char-à-Banc was essentially a country vehicle for use in large establishments where there would be a need to convey a number of people and a quantity of luggage on occasions such as a shooting party.

In some Char-à-Bancs the seats were reached by means of steps which folded and then slid into the boot where they were hidden by a small door. Others were entered through doors and the folding steps were not completely hidden. A few had a rear staircase which led to the high seats at the back of the vehicle.

Canopies were erected on some to protect passengers from the weather.

Varieties of springing were used. Some were built on a perch and mail springs, others had elliptic springs.

It was said that Char-à-Bancs were constructed in more forms than most other carriages. The seating arrangements varied enormously but all carried a large number of travellers.

The vehicle was favoured by the young for trying their hand at driving a team, owing to its road-holding capacities. Some proprietors, who were anxious to cash in on this virtue, began to refer to the vehicle as a coach and even went to the extreme lengths of fitting dummy bodies onto their Char-à-Bancs. It was not long before these vehicles had earned the name of Bastard Coaches.

As time progressed, Char-à-Bancs were produced in colourful editions to be used as sightseeing vehicles.

The Char-à-Banc illustrated here was built around 1890 by S. Mitchell. It is known as the 'Ardrishaig Belle' and was used with a pair at Ardrishaig, Argyll, up to the 1950s. It has accommodation for sixteen people. This Char-à-Banc may be seen in the Museum of Transport, Glasgow, Scotland, where it was acquired from Mr A. R. Grinlaw of Ardrishaig in 1961.

The word Char-à-Banc is nowadays loosely applied to a tourist coach.

Above: Char-à-Banc
Left: Roof-Seat Break

ROOF-SEAT BREAK

The threequarter-size Roof-Seat Break shown on the previous page was built for the author's pony team in 1978 by John Gapp of Dereham, Norfolk, England, on traditional lines.

There is accommodation for six people on the forward-facing seats.

The hind boot is reached by a door at the back, which is hinged at the bottom. Access to the front boot is gained through a trap door in the floor by the box seat.

The splinter bar has been made on the lines of one which is described in Fairman Roger's *Manual of Coaching*. Each horse's traces are attached to roller bolts at either end of a pivoting swingle tree which, at first glance, resembles a splinter bar. This arrangement makes the draught more comfortable for the wheelers.

The brake is both hand and foot operated onto the front of the rear wheels.

HRH THE DUKE OF EDINBURGH'S FIRST COMPETITION CARRIAGE

HRH The Duke of Edinburgh's First Competition Carriage

Built in 1974 by Henry Bowers of Chard, Somerset, England, the wheels, undercarriage and frame of the body are of all metal

construction; the body itself is made of panels of marine ply which can be easily replaced. This was the first competition carriage to be specially designed and built and has served as the prototype for many others which have been and are now being built.

HRH THE DUKE OF EDINBURGH'S PHAETON
(see colour illustration facing page 161)

This carriage was built by Artistic Iron Products of Long Bennington, Newark, Nottinghamshire, England, in 1979, to the design of HRH The Duke of Edinburgh.

The vehicle combines the smart appearance of a traditional carriage for the presentation and dressage phases of a combined driving event with the ruggedness which is essential for the cross-country phase. It has a number of special features which make it suitable for this purpose.

The body is built on a steel frame which is clad with a special type of plywood imported from Sweden. The top surface is covered with paper giving a first-class base onto which the ten-coat paint finish is applied.

The doors of the body are removable so that they can be taken off for the marathon section to enable the grooms to dismount quickly if the need arises.

The disc brakes can be both hand and foot operated.

The pole is made of steel and the bars of aluminium.

The steel wheels are mounted on axles which are adjustable for width. They can be narrowed for the cross-country phase when there is need to negotiate the four-in-hand team through tight gateways and similar hazards. The hub caps, too, are flat for this reason. The axles are widened for the obstacle competition to give a wheel track of 160cms which is the maximum width permitted. The cones on the course are altered as necessary to allow the same clearance for all competitors between the outside track width of their wheels and the obstacle.

KIRKBRIK (CHURCH BREAK)

The Kirkbrik (or Church Break) is a Dutch vehicle which was used for taking the family to church.

There were two kinds: those used by Roman Catholics which had two seats inside the length of the vehicle, and those used by Protestants or Calvinists which had one long seat and one small seat which could only be used for children. Apparently, this seating arrangement was chosen so that one passenger would not touch the knees of another whilst going to church.

Kirkbrik or Church Break

The vehicle which is illustrated here forms part of Mr W. Bakker's collection in Holland.

WAGONETTE

The Wagonette is a country vehicle from which it is possible to drive a single, pair, unicorn or team from the high box seat. Passengers can be accommodated on the inward-facing bench seats at the rear, which are reached by a door at the back of the vehicle. Wagonettes were popular in the nineteenth century for conveying passengers and luggage, owing to the amount of space available.

They are now in demand for present-day driving activities and English examples are becoming hard to find. During the past decade, numerous wagonettes have been imported into Britain from the Continent. These are frequently fitted with swingle trees instead of a fixed splinter bar and roller bolts which are usually found on English-built editions.

This fine vehicle was built by the London coachbuilder Offord, and is in Mrs John Gordon's collection at Stratford St Mary, Suffolk, England.

There are two interesting features of this carriage. One is that the floorboards can be lifted to reveal a well which is suitable for carrying guns and game, and the other is that the longitudinal inward-facing rear seats can be moved to become forward-facing bench seats.

Wagonette

WAGONETTE BREAK

The Wagonette Break is a larger version of the wagonette and is usually driven with a pair, unicorn or team. Some Wagonette Breaks have a second seat which is similar to, and situated behind, the front seat to take three or even four more passengers. The rear bench seats of these large vehicles would accommodate six or eight more travellers, making the vehicle popular for such pursuits as attending coursing or hunt race meetings. The carriage was equally useful for collecting luggage from stations or conveying servants.

Large Wagonette Breaks are sometimes referred to as Body Breaks and are very useful for exercising and for training teams of coach horses.

The vehicle illustrated is in Mr and Mrs Sanders Watney's collection and can be seen at Breamore House, Hampshire, England.

Wagonette Break

JERSEY VAN

The Jersey Van is a four-wheeled open dray which is used in the Channel Island of Jersey for carrying produce, such as potatoes, down from the farms to merchants on the coast for shipping to the English mainland.

The solid body is frequently highly painted. It is built on a substantial frame and has five panels. Two bench seats on either side of the body make the van an ideal vehicle for taking tourists on sightseeing trips of the Island.

Many Jersey Vans have two brakes operating on the rear wheels. A screw-on lever, which is placed to the right of the driver, is used for securing the vehicle on a hill and works on blocks at the front of the wheels. A foot brake operates blocks on the backs of the wheels and is used for braking when descending a hill or stopping in a crowded street.

The single or pair of vanner-type horses are driven from a forward-facing bench seat.

The Jersey Van illustrated here is owned and driven by Mr Surcouf.

A Guernsey Van is similar to a Jersey Van but is slightly smaller and lighter, having just four body panels on each side.

The Sark Van is a modern vehicle which is found on the Channel

Island of Sark where the only motorized vehicles allowed are tractors, which are used for such duties as conveying passengers and luggage up the long steep hill from the boat.

The Sark Van has evolved from the Jersey and Guernsey Vans in response to tourist demands.

The metalwork of Sark Vans comes from old Jersey or Guernsey Vans. These are broken down and rebuilt on Sark into a more practical size for carrying people on sightseeing tours round the narrow lanes of the Island. The heavy, solid wooden bodies which were needed for the transport of weighty farm produce are replaced by substantial frames supporting lightweight bodywork. The upper limit of passengers on a Sark public vehicle is ten, so the vans are designed to seat eight on longitudinal, inward-facing bench seats, which are reached by a rear door, and two more tourists are seated alongside the driver on the forward-facing box seat.

The braking system varies. Some vans have foot brakes, but most have a wind-on brake which is operated by a small handle placed to the right of the driver's seat.

Most Sark Vans are rubber shod. This increases the comfort of passengers and also makes it possible for them to hear the driver's commentary as he describes places of interest along the route. A few vans are iron shod but they are not favoured owing to the amount of damage which they cause to Sark's unmade roads in wet weather. There is no wheelwright living on Sark. The wheels are made in England. At the end

Jersey Van

Summer Break

of the summer season, a cargo boat transports large numbers of wheels for repairs during the winter months by mainland craftsmen.

SUMMER BREAK

The Summer Break (Zomerbrik) is a typically Dutch carriage.

The wagonette-type body is fitted with tilts which can be unrolled to protect travellers if the weather is bad.

This vehicle forms a part of Mr W. Bakker's collection in Holland.

LONSDALE BREAK

OPPOSITE
Above: Canadian Caleche
Below: Indian Cart or
Tonga

The Lonsdale Wagonette is a wagonette which has the usual seating arrangement covered with two folding leather heads opening longitudinally.

There are doubts regarding the credit for the invention. A Mr

Robertson claimed to have built a wagonette on those lines in 1864, whilst a Mr Kinder is said to have constructed one a year later. The famous coachbuilders, Messrs Morgan, are reported to have produced such a carriage in 1870. However, in 1893 Lord Lonsdale presented a Landau 'Wagonette' to the Duke and Duchess of York on their marriage and allowed his name to be given to the vehicle as he assumed that he was the first person to use a head which folded over the wheels instead of fore and aft.

Whatever the origin, the vehicle became popular and the name remained.

One was exhibited by Mr Hamshaw of Leicester at the Royal Agricultural Society's Show in 1896 and since then a version was built by this craftsman for the Prince of Wales.

The Lonsdale Wagonette seen here was built in about 1900 by Hamshaw and can be viewed in the Museum of Transport, Glasgow, Scotland, where it is on loan from John Shand Ltd.

UTRECHT TENT WAGON (UTRECHTSE TENTWAGEN)

A typically Dutch vehicle, the one illustrated overleaf being a comparatively late model.

OPPOSITE
Above: Country Cart
Below: HRH The Duke of Edinburgh's Phaeton

Lonsdale Wagonette

Utrecht Tent Wagon

Earlier tent wagons were open sided, having curtains which could be dropped down from the canopy-type top to the curving sides. These wagons had windows but no doors at the sides. Entry was made from the front of the vehicle via the box seat.

The carriage which is shown here is a more sophisticated version, having doors and windows at the sides and a hood which gives greater protection against the weather. Passengers mount from steps by the doors.

The wagon belongs to Mr J. A. Hamann, Vorden, Netherlands.

OMNIBUSES

The use of the word 'Omnibus' was first recorded in England in 1829, in reference to a vehicle, when George Shillibeer informed the Chairman of the Board of Stamps that he was intending to start an Omnibus service.

The idea had been conceived by Monsieur Jacques Lafitte in 1819 when he decided to introduce, in France, an alternative passenger-carrying vehicle to the usual coaches and carts.

A man named Baudry was, at that time, using coaches to transport passengers to a public baths which he owned. Across the road from the baths was a shop owned by a tradesman known as Omnes. Above the door of the shop hung a sign saying 'Omnes Omnibus – All things for Everybody'. Baudry took the name Omnibus for his coaches and wrote it on the sides of his vehicles. They became generally known as Baudry's Omnibuses.

Jacques Lafitte liked the idea and also called his passenger vehicle an Omnibus.

At that time George Shillibeer was working as a coachbuilder in Paris. He built a version of the Omnibus for Lafitte and then decided to go to London where he planned to make his fortune with Omnibuses in the big city.

On 4th July 1829, Shillibeer's first Omnibus was launched. It seated about eighteen passengers on the inward-facing, longitudinal, inside benches and was entered by a door at the back. Three horses were put to, alongside each other, to draw the Omnibus between Paddington Green and The Bank.

The advantages claimed were that passengers could be picked up and put down easily along the route. Up to that time the only public transport in and around the metropolis was by short stage carriages running from one inn to another. They were not allowed to stop in the paved streets of built-up areas. The use of an Omnibus was more convenient because tickets did not have to be bought at booking offices and long waits at The Cellar (Hatchetts, The White Horse Cellar, Piccadilly, which was the starting point for numerous coaches) were avoided.

These first Omnibuses were manned by fellow shipmates from Shillibeer's earlier days in the Royal Navy. This was not a success. The men soon grew bored and crafty. They took to pocketing a large proportion of the fares. These men were replaced by high-quality coachmen who became well known for their smart dress and courtesy to travellers.

Shillibeer provided books in his buses to prevent passengers from boredom.

The service grew and gradually smaller two-horse buses were put on the road both by Shillibeer and by other proprietors. Although the name Omnibus was employed generally, Shillibeer used his own name, written on the side of the bus, as a fleet title and people often referred to 'taking a Shillibeer' when travelling by bus. Unfortunately for this originator, his business did not last. Rival firms sprang up all over the country. Drivers stole his fares in spite of Shillibeer's efforts to have them watched by inspectors. Passengers borrowed books from his library in order to finish the story and did not bother to return them. Proprietors with few morals had written in small letters the words 'not the original' in front of the large 'Shillibeer' on the sides of their vehicles so that passengers who had hurried to catch a Shillibeer found, on entering, that the bus was not of the expected high standard. After about six years Shillibeer was forced off the road. He started an undertakers business. The hearses had 'Shillibeer's Funeral Carriages' written on their sides. People no longer liked to talk of 'taking a Shillibeer' and said that they were going by Omnibus.

Methods of carrying passengers on the roofs of Omnibuses improved gradually. At first, two or three people were permitted to ride alongside the driver. Then a seat was put behind the driver for more travellers. By 1845 it was customary for male passengers to perch on the curved roof, sitting back to back, when rush-hour travel forced them to do so. By 1847 roof-seat travel was being encouraged by halving the fare. The roof was reached by iron rungs.

The first Knifeboard Omnibus was so named in 1852. A plank was bolted along the roof and people sat, back to back, facing the sides of the road, leaning against the board. It was said to resemble the old knife-cleaning boards which were used with emery powder for cleaning steel knives.

In 1855, the London General Omnibus Company was started. It took over as many of London's bus proprietors as was possible and soon owned threequarters of London's buses.

In 1856 a premium of £100 was offered for 'the best design and specification for an omnibus that with the same weight as at present will afford increased space, accommodation and comfort to the public'. Seventy-five entries were submitted. Mr R. F. Miller's design was the one which the judges considered to be of the greatest value. They found that a combination of ideas from many of the designers aided the production of a suitable vehicle.

The standard double-deck bus had back-to-back longitudinal seats on the roof to accommodate five passengers on each side. Two people sat on either side of the driver. There was seating inside for twelve travellers bringing the total carried to twenty-six.

The wheels of all the buses were painted yellow which simplified repairs and replacements.

By the 1860s a few daring ladies had ventured onto the roof seats. Modesty or decency boards were fixed to obliterate the view of these travellers' ankles from the ground. These boards were subsequently used for advertising.

Brakes were not generally employed until the 1870s. They were then foot operated. Buses on the Continent were fitted with the wheel type of screw-on brake.

The Garden Seat Omnibus was introduced in 1881 by the London Road-Car Company Limited. These seats were acceptable for the use of ladies owing to the improved access by a front staircase. The forward-facing seats were also more popular. The vehicle was standardized and used generally to the end of the horse bus era by London proprietors. It

accommodated fourteen people who sat in pairs on the roof seats and twelve more passengers who rode inside.

By 1905 there were over 1,400 Omnibuses and 17,000 horses working in London for the London General Omnibus Company. The total number of horse buses which were licensed in London at that time was nearly 3,500.

The first of the London General Omnibus Company horse buses was withdrawn from service in 1906 and the last in 1911, though other proprietors continued for a few more years.

The last horse buses which were on regular routes in London, operated by Tilling, were withdrawn in 1914 due to requisitioning of horses for World War I.

One hundred and fifty years after the first Omnibus was put on the road, in July 1979, a fifty-year-old replica headed an anniversary cavalcade, followed by Garden Seat and Knifeboard buses, along the old route of Moorgate, City Road, Pentonville, Euston and Marylebone Roads.

A horse bus service ran between Baker Street and London Zoo from 2nd July to the end of September 1979, as a tourist attraction.

SHILLIBEER OMNIBUS

(see colour illustration facing page 176)

This bus can be seen in the London Transport Museum, Covent Garden, London, WC2.

KNIFEBOARD OMNIBUS

This bus (illustrated on preceding page) can be seen in the London Transport Museum, Covent Garden, London, WC2.

GARDEN-SEAT OMNIBUS

This bus can be seen in the London Transport Museum, Covent Garden, London, WC2.

PRIVATE OMNIBUS

The Private Omnibus was first used in England in the 1860s.
It was one of the most popular informal carriages and considered to be

Garden-Seat Omnibus

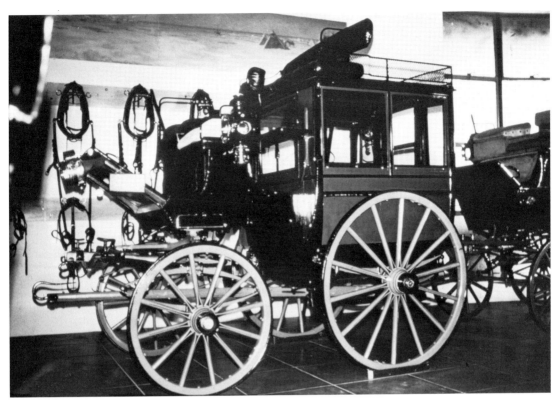

Private Omnibus

an indispensable vehicle for a large establishment.

The rear accommodation carried four to six people on inward-facing seats which were reached by a door at the back. The rear step was kept free from mud by a plate which opened with the door. The closed body protected passengers from the weather whilst the front and side windows permitted plenty of light. Some were fitted with external lamps which lit up the inside of the carriage. Internal fittings on many were numerous. They included hat nets and umbrella straps as well as cupboards and pockets for such items as packs of cards and books.

In 1897 Mr Cremmen of Kentish Town, London, devised a ventilation system with apertures under the roof. Up to that time sliding windows were all that had been available.

Some Private Omnibuses had rear seats for footmen on either side of the door. Many had an outside seat at the front of the roof, behind the box seat, which accommodated up to four people depending on the size of the carriage.

Light editions were built for use with a single horse whilst others were made for pair, unicorn (two wheelers and one leader), or even a team. The suspension frequently consisted of two pairs of full elliptic springs in front and side springs at the rear.

The Omnibus was often used for station and theatre work, which earned it the names of Station Bus and Opera Bus.

Sometimes it would be used for sporting occasions such as a visit to the races. Here it acted as a first-class grandstand with the additional luxury of inside seating if the weather was cold and there was a need to get out of the wind between races. Lunch could also be eaten in comfort when a folding table would be erected between the bench seats. This arrangement would have been comparable to a twentieth-century caravan being towed by a Land Rover with roof seats.

A few Private Omnibuses were built so that the top could be removed to convert the carriage into a wagonette. There exists, in at least one Suffolk coach house, the pulleys on the roof with which, it is stated by those who remember, 'they used to take the top off the Omnibus'.

The Private Omnibus illustrated can be seen in El Pomar Carriage House, Colorado Springs, Colorado, USA. It was built in 1890 by Million Guiet of Paris, France, and purchased by Chester A. Arthur (the son of the twenty-first President of the United States) in 1902 in Paris, who then brought the vehicle to the United States. This Omnibus is painted in the colours of the Parisian Carriage Club of which Mr Arthur was a member. It has presto lights and the gas tank is under the driver's seat. The vehicle was used for taking guests to the opera and to concerts.

CONTINENTAL PRIVATE OMNIBUS

This Omnibus was built by Vanden Plas in Belgium. It is suitable for an owner driving his horses to a sporting event as there are two seats at the back for grooms.

The carriage forms part of Baron Casier's collection in Belgium.

STATION BUS

The Station Bus was a commercialized edition of the Private Omnibus. Such a vehicle found favour amongst hotel owners for transporting visitors to and from stations.

This vehicle was built by the famous Glasgow coachbuilding firm of Hendersons around 1900. It accommodated six passengers on the longitudinal seats inside and two more people behind the box seats. Luggage was carried on the roof.

It can be seen in the Museum of Transport in Glasgow, Scotland, by whom it was acquired from Mr J. Lawson in 1964.

OPPOSITE
Above: Continental
Private Omnibus
Below: Station Bus

HEARSE

Hearses were constructed in large numbers with varying degrees of grandeur. Some were plainly built affairs whilst others were ornately carved and highly decorated. They were always painted black, except those which carried children which were finished in white.

Hearses were drawn by pairs or four-in-hand teams of black horses known as the 'Black Brigade'. These animals were usually stallions of the Flemish breed. They were beautifully turned out in black harness which was decorated with black plumes.

The hearse illustrated here, which was built in Greenock, Scotland, in 1875, can be seen in the Museum of Transport, Glasgow, Scotland. It was acquired from Mr A. R. Grinlaw, Ardrishaig, in 1961.

SLEIGH

This English sleigh is driven from the front seat. The rumble seat at the rear accommodates the groom or third traveller. The shafts have hooks at their ends which slot into the rings above the runners. The high rein rail is constructed to hold the reins well clear of the horse's tail.

One of the worst hazards of sleigh driving is the bombardment of clods

Hearse

Sleigh

of snow which are sometimes thrown into the passengers' faces from the horse's feet. This is why so many sleighs have high curving dash boards.

It is found that this sleigh runs better when there is a passenger on the rumble as his weight lightens the front of the runners.

The sleigh illustrated here is in the author's collection.

Part V
COACHES, WAGONS AND COACHMAN-DRIVEN VEHICLES

COACHES

The word 'coach' is thought to have originated from the Hungarian town of Kotze where it is claimed that the first coach was built.

The term coach is now normally applied to a four-wheeled enclosed carriage, in which the roof forms part of the framing of the body, with interior seating provided for four people. If there is only inside accommodation for two, facing forward, then the vehicle is more usually called a chariot.

Queen Mary Tudor travelled in a four-wheeled chariot, drawn by six horses, to her coronation in 1553.

Some authorities state that the first coach, as opposed to a chariot, was made in England in 1555. The vehicle was built for the Earl of Rutland by Walter Rippon who also made a coach for Queen Mary in 1556.

Other historians claim that the first coach ever to be seen in England was one which was brought from Holland by William Booner, a Dutchman, for Queen Elizabeth I in 1560, according to some authorities, and 1564 according to others.

The first English state coach was built in 1564 by Walter Rippon and used for the Opening of Parliament in 1571. It was said, by some, that the Queen suffered so much in this vehicle on that occasion, that she never used it again, preferring Booner's coach.

By the end of the decade, coaches were being used by those whose purses could stretch to such extravagance.

Concern arose over the use of coaches. They were considered to be rather effeminate and it was feared that men would lose their capabilities as horsemen if they persisted in riding about in coaches instead of on their horses' backs. A Bill was read in Parliament in 1601 to curb the use of coaches but was rejected.

By 1640, stage coaches were in use. They were employed for conveying passengers and goods between London and the larger towns. Roads were almost non-existent so travel was slow and uncomfortable. Vehicles were virtually unsprung. Average speeds of three miles an hour were normal. These conveyances were known as 'Flying Wagons' as they were considerably faster than pack horses. The wagons were constructed with wheels which resembled road rollers. It was thought that these would improve the unmade tracks and prevent the wagon from becoming bogged down. In fact, in soft conditions, they dug deep furrows making the road worse for any traffic which followed.

Hackney coaches plied for hire in London in the early seventeenth century. By 1634 a stand was formed in London's Strand. A year later, there were reports of traffic jams in the City and Charles I prevented their use unless a journey of three or more miles was to be made out of London. By 1660 they were considered to be a public nuisance and were not allowed to stand in the street. They had to remain in their yards until they

174

were wanted. Eventually, laws were passed and hackney coaches operated by a limited number of licences. This, understandably, led to a variety of devious practices such as pirate cabmen plying for hire by night when they hoped to escape from notice of the commissioners.

A cumbersome, postillion-driven coach was in use by 1663. This had sideways-facing seats in the doorways on which travellers, mostly of low rank, rode. Their legs and feet fitted into boxes which were commonly called 'boots'. It is from this that the term boot was derived.

The first toll gate appeared on the Great North Road in 1663 in order to collect money to repair the Cambridgeshire, Hertfordshire and Huntingdonshire road which had become 'ruinous and almost impassable'. At first, the idea was very unpopular but became more acceptable as it was realized that the revenue which was gathered resulted in better roads and faster travel.

Up to this time coaches had no proper springs and had only been, at their best, hung on leather braces from iron shackles.

In 1665 Samuel Pepys wrote in his diary that Colonel Blunt (or Blount) had introduced a carriage which was fitted with springs but that it was 'not so easy as he pretends'.

There are records of coaches being hung on leather straps from a type of elbow spring at each corner instead of just directly to iron shackles.

After 1666, when the Great Fire of London had devastated the city, the streets were widened and traffic jams lessened. More licences were issued for hackney coaches.

By the early eighteenth century, the turnpike system had led to great advances in coaching. Builders applied their skills to produce better vehicles. Lighter horses were bred and put to the coaches. There were, however, still many horrific conditions which had to be negotiated. It is hard to believe that there could have been, in 1736, an impassable gulf of mud between Kensington and London, but this was so.

In 1768, awards were presented by the Society of English Arts and Manufacturers for an invention of springing to Dr R. Lovell Edgeworth.

Whip springs were found to be satisfactory and a great relief to passengers and horses. Springs resembling whip springs but with slightly more curved outline were also used and were known as S-springs. Braces were fixed between the corners of the body of the coach and the tops of the whip or S-springs.

By the end of the seventeen-hundreds, cee-springs were being used. They gave even greater comfort. Lighter carriages were constructed.

Up to this time, many carriages had been built on a single or double perch undercarriage. The latter was known as a Berlin undercarriage. Early Berlins were built with small front wheels enabling them to turn under their perches. Crane-neck perched undercarriages were constructed to allow larger front wheels to turn under the arch so that full lock could be obtained with bigger wheels.

In 1802, the elliptic spring was invented by Obadiah Elliott, allowing coaches to be built without the use of a perch. It was employed in 1804 and is now found on numerous carriages. The elliptic spring forms an oval outline and is made from two side springs. The axle is usually connected to the lower spring with U-bolts and the upper half of the spring is normally fixed to the body of the vehicle. This invention revolutionized the coachbuilding trade.

The 'golden age of coaching' lasted only for the quarter century between 1815 and 1840, during which time the stage and mail coaches reached the height of their perfection due to the great improvements which were made to the roads by John MacAdam's and Telford's system of surfacing.

This 'golden age' ended due to competition from the railways.

QUALIFICATIONS OF A GOOD COACHMAN

Quoted from Underhill's *Driving for Pleasure*, 1896

'The town coachman must be a man of experience, and reasonable wages paid to such a man will often save a large expenditure in paint and repairs. The thorough coachman can be distinguished at a glance, and it is unfortunate that they are so few and far between.'

COACH OF PHILIP II OF SPAIN

This carriage was built in Spain at the end of the sixteenth century and brought to Portugal in 1619 by Philip II.

The outside is covered in leather and decorated with studs. The luggage trunk at the front is also of leather and similarly studded.

The vehicle was drawn by postillion-driven horses.

This coach can be seen in the National Coach Museum at Lisbon.

MAIL COACH

OPPOSITE
Above: Shillibeer Omnibus
Below: Cobb & Co Coach

Mail Coaches began running at the end of the seventeen-hundreds to replace the existing postboys who were frequently stopped by highwaymen.

By 1835, there were said to be about seven hundred mail coaches

Coach of Philip II of Spain

covering regular routes. They were built on a perch undercarriage with telegraph springs and mail axles.

The armed guard sat on a single seat, over the hind boot, which was opened by a hinged door under his feet so that no one could get to the boot without first removing him. A tool kit, in which was kept a blunderbuss and a pair of pistols, was fixed to the roof in front of the guard.

There was outside accommodation for four passengers as well as the coachman. Four more travellers rode inside.

All mail coaches were painted black with scarlet wheels and undercarriages and maroon lower body and door panels with 'GR' or 'VR', depending on the year, on the sides of the front boot. The number of the coach was inscribed on the sides of the hind boot. The words 'Royal Mail' were painted on the door panels as were the two towns between which the coach ran. The upper quarter panels of the coach were decorated with the four stars of the Order of Knighthood on their black surfaces. The stars of Bath and St Patrick embellished the offside, and those of the Garter and Thistle were painted on the nearside.

Mail coaches had right of way over everyone else on the road. Toll gates had to be flung open to allow them through without delay as they

OPPOSITE
Above: Lucy Coach
Below: Cipriani panel on Gold State Coach

Mail Coach

179

paid no tolls. The timing of the mail was split second and it was said that villagers could set their watches at the passing of these coaches.

The mail coach illustrated can be seen in the Science Museum, London, and is said to have been built by Messrs Ward(e) and Co in about 1820.

ROAD COACH

The name 'Road Coach' was given, in the 1860s at the time of the coaching revival, to coaches which had previously been known as stage coaches, in order to differentiate them from private coaches.

The first stage coaches ran in the sixteen-hundreds during the summer months when tracks were passable. The dangers of coach travel were many and varied. It is no wonder that fond farewells and prayers were said, and wills were written before embarking on a long journey. The likelihood of being held up by a highwayman or meeting with an accident due to the appalling condition of some of the roads was considerable.

Public coaches ran on regular routes at set times. They conveyed four passengers inside and twelve outside as well as the professional coachman and the scarlet-coated guard. The latter travelled on the nearside of the rear seat which held four people. From this position, he was able to reach down to open the door of the hind boot which is hinged on the offside for this reason. It was the guard's job to look after passengers' seating arrangements, attend to their luggage, keep the coach running to time, and carry out such jobs as applying the skid pan to a rear wheel at the top of steep hills and removing it at the bottom.

Long distances were frequently covered. Journeys were made up by a series of stages with numerous changes of horses at coaching inns along the road. The distance of a stage depended largely on the terrain and the speed at which the horses were driven, but it would have been between five and fifteen miles. Two or three minutes was considered to be adequate for a normal change of teams though the time taken for a quick change was under a minute.

Road coaches were constructed by many of the leading carriage builders such as Holland and Holland, and Shanks. The coaches were of a robust nature to cope with the considerable milage and daily use. They weighed about a ton and were painted in bright colours. The main towns and inns visited were written on the side panels and boots. The name of the coach was inscribed in large letters on the back of the rumble above the hind boot panel and frequently on the underneath of the footboard. Such titles as 'Old Times', 'Telegraph' and 'Rocket' were given to road coaches. Many are still in existence in various parts of the world.

A net of leather straps was fastened between the roof seats, on which could be placed small parcels and passengers' coats.

Road Coach

A wooden folding ladder was fixed to the hind boot in readiness for the guard to erect if required by passengers on the roof seats.

A leather horn case was strapped to the nearside where it could be reached by the guard. It was customary for him to blow the horn both to warn ostlers of the approaching coach and to clear the road in towns where sharp, blind corners had to be negotiated.

Then, the coming of the railways brought a rapid decline to coach travel.

However, in 1860 amateur coachmen began to take an interest in the art of handling four horses and a few stage coaches were put on the road in the summer. These were run by syndicates who got together to raise the necessary funds to keep them going.

The 'Red Rover' road coach illustrated here was built by Shanks. It ran between London and Southampton until 1843, carrying passengers and their luggage. Then, during the coaching revival it ran between Margate and Herne Bay from about 1890 until World War I. In 1948 it was acquired and restored by Mr Sanders Watney. Between 1952 and 1965 it ran four days each summer alternately to Southampton and Brighton from London.

It was also driven at shows with considerable success in coaching marathons by both Mr Sanders Watney and Mr Jim Corbett.

Private Coach

The 'Red Rover' can now be seen at Breamore House in Hampshire, England, where it forms part of Mr and Mrs Sanders Watney's collection.

PRIVATE COACH

A Private Coach is sometimes called a Private Drag or Park Drag. It is a lighter version of a road coach.

Private coaches have a more refined finish than road coaches and they are frequently adorned with discrete carving of the wood on the undercarriage. The shackles at the ends of the springs are often covered in leather. The outside seating is for two less than that of a road coach because the rumble (rear) seat, on iron stays, is built to carry only the two grooms. The 'lazy' backs of the central roof seats are designed to fold so that they can be flattened when no passengers are carried. The luggage or picnic box which is sometimes stowed between these seats is known as the Imperial.

The hind boot of a private coach is hinged at the bottom so that the door can be let down on quadrants to form a table. Zinc-lined mahogany lunchboxes can then be pulled out onto the flat surface for serving.

The front boot, which is frequently reached from inside the coach, contains such items as headcollars, rugs and similar equipment.

It is normal to carry spare lead and main bars on the rear of the coach, and a folding iron ladder under the grooms' seat. Some coaches carry a spare pole alongside the perch. This was made from three sections which could be screwed together and held in place by metal collars.

A jointed whip on a board was sometimes taken on a drag.

The horn case was made of basket work.

Private coaches were built for use by gentlemen who wished to drive their own four-in-hand teams for pleasure. These vehicles were employed for attending such functions as race meetings when the outside seating formed an ideal grandstand.

The body was painted in a more sombre hue than that of a mail or road coach, possibly in the family colours. Lining was kept to a minimum with just a single stripe where applicable. The owner's crest or monogram would discreetly adorn the crest panels on the doors and the hind boot. The iron work was black so that it could easily be touched up when it became scratched.

The private coach illustrated here was built by the English coachbuilders, Holland and Holland. It was said to have been used by the twentieth Earl of Shrewsbury on his favourite drive from Ingestre to Buxton and back via Alton. This coach was purchased by the Staffordshire County Museum in 1964 from Lord Shrewsbury and can now be seen there at Shugborough, Stafford, England.

CONCORD COACH

The Concord Coach is an American coach which took its name from the town of Concord in New Hampshire, USA, where over six hundred were built by the famous firm of Abbot and Downing.

By 1830 Abbot and Downing considered that they had developed a design to perfect the Concord.

By the end of the nineteenth century it was claimed that about three thousand had been made by various coachbuilders.

Concords were used extensively on both mail and stage lines all over the United States and South America, being built for business purposes on rough roads. It was said that they could bear any amount of hard usage and run safely over roads which would have dislocated an English coach in the first half mile.

An Abbot-Downing coach earned a high reputation. It was claimed that 'it don't break down but only wears out'. Mark Twain is reputed to have described the Concord as 'an imposing cradle on wheels' owing, no doubt, to its mode of suspension.

Stage-coach operators advertized the fact that they used 'Concord coaches along with their best horses and careful drivers'.

They varied considerably in construction. Some Concords were heavy-duty vehicles made for use in the Western States and Territories. Several were exported to South Africa and Australia. Lighter versions were in use in the White Mountain areas.

Many were built to seat nine people inside whilst others were made to take as many as thirty-one travellers behind six horses.

Generally, the frame and body were made of oak and the wheels of ash. The undercarriage, which was often painted yellow, consisted of three parallel perches between the front transom bed and the hind axle.

The body was hung on thick leather thoroughbraces which formed the suspension. It was claimed that these could be replaced by the roughest workmen. Four iron standards coming from the corners of the undercarriage frame supported the thoroughbraces with square iron shackles. Excess sideways motion was prevented by straps going from the side perches to the lower part of the coach. The fore and aft body sway was said to be likely to make a sensitive person travel-sick.

The rocking of the coach caused the driver's hands to be in perpetual forward and backward motion which prevented the Concord from being driven for amateur pleasure purposes adopting the fine driving method with the reins held 'English style'.

Concord Coach

The brake was attached to the undercarriage and was operated by the driver's right foot on a crossbar which pressed the lever forward to push the brake blocks against the rear wheels. There was no ratchet so the lever had to be held in position by the foot. This, too, prevented any possibility of elegant driving.

The traces were fixed to swingle trees which were in turn shackled to a central evener.

Some Concords had glass windows at the sides whilst others had roll up leather curtains on each side of the door with just narrow windows between the door and the curtains.

Passengers' luggage was carried in leather covered trunks at the rear of the coach as well as under the driver's seat and on the roof.

The Concord Coach illustrated was built in 1866 by the Abbot Downing Company. It bears the serial number 117. The photograph is reproduced by courtesy of Carling O'Keefe Breweries of Canada Limited, Toronto, Canada.

COBB & CO COACH

(see colour illustration facing page 176)

Cobb & Co Coaches first appeared in Australia in 1854. The firm was founded by four enterprising young Americans, namely Freeman Cobb, John B. Lamber, John Murray Peck and James Swanton.

The gold rush in the early 1850s created a transport problem for the thousands of men who poured inland in search of riches. The situation provided an opportunity for someone to start a coach service. The vehicles had to combine the qualities of speed with reliability. The rough tracks over which the coaches were expected to travel demanded a rugged design. They had to carry passengers as well as their luggage and the gold which they mined.

English coaches had been tried but were found to be unsuitable. The metal springs did not stand up to the constant battering which they received on the rough roads.

The American Concord Coach was discovered to be suitable because of its thoroughbrace mode of suspension. This reduced the shocks to passengers and made it easier for the horses as the body swayed backwards and forwards lessening the concussion on the wheels when they hit a rut. The coach was built with a rounded, egg-shaped body. It could be drawn by four, six or eight horses and was usually driven by American coachmen.

Freeman Cobb and his partners first imported Concord Coaches from America in 1853 and started a service between Melbourne and the gold fields. This was an instant success.

Soon, the coaches became known as Cobb & Co Coaches serving as the only public coaches to and from the gold mining areas.

By the end of the century, the word 'Cobb' was generally accepted (in Australia) as a noun meaning coach.

In 1856, the firm sold out and Freeman Cobb and John Lamber returned to America but the name was already established and therefore retained by the men who ran the business along the same lines as their predecessors. Swanton and Peck kept up their coaching connections in Australia, at the time.

Most of the Concord Coaches were yellow. In about 1862 Cobb & Co Coaches were first painted with the dark red bodies, gold lettering and cream undercarriage which later became familiar with travellers. At that time, James Rutherford took over control of Cobb & Co. He continued this service, as links with the railways, for fifty years. Rutherford ordered two coaches to be built by a Bathurst, New South Wales, firm and it is said that because he failed to specify the colour required they painted the coaches dark red.

These Cobb Coaches were modified versions of Concords. They were built in Bathurst, New South Wales, and Brisbane, Queensland, as well as at Charleville in Queensland. After 1890, they were all built at Charleville. The coaches were finished with a more rugged design. The curving body was replaced by a rectangular construction with a flat floor. These coaches were obviously more solidly built than they appear because considerable loads were stacked onto their roofs without damage to the vehicles. A box with a hinged lid was built under the driver's seat and used for carrying gold. This was apparently frequently buried under hundredweight bags of wheat to make it difficult for bushrangers (highwaymen) to relieve the travellers of their riches. Two sizes of coaches were 'standard' at the Charleville factory. The smaller eight-passenger coach cost £175 in 1913 and the larger fourteen-passenger vehicle sold for £210. The eight-seater carried four people inside and took two on the rear-facing roof seat and two more alongside the driver on a seat which overlapped the body. The fourteen-seat coach had accommodation for nine inside on three rows of sparsely padded bench seats. The middle seat, which was placed aft of the door, had a pull-down back to allow passengers to climb over onto the rear seat. Two people travelled alongside the driver and three more sat on the rear outside seat. Leather blinds protected the inside passengers. Some coaches had a folding hood over the driver's seat to give cover to these travellers from the sun. On some, there was an apron which pulled up over their legs to give protection against rain. The body was hung on thoroughbraces which were made of buffalo hide. They had a turnbuckle below the doorway to enable the braces to be tightened as necessary. The Charleville coaches were painted white with red letters. They were drawn by teams of five (two wheelers and three leaders) or seven (four wheelers and three leaders).

Coach travellers had a choice of enduring the cold, wet or heat of outside seats or the combination of draught or partial suffocation and travel-sickness on the inside ones. The dangers of robbery were considerable as were those of accident. Mountains, deserts and bush had to be negotiated. In spite of all the disadvantages, travellers throughout New South Wales and Queensland relied on Cobb & Co to link the rail system and to carry freight and mail.

Laws were laid down to try to prevent accidents due to overloading coaches. One rule specified by the proprietors of Cobb & Co in the Victorian era, was 'no ladies allowed on the box seat of the coach'. A fine of forty shillings was payable by the driver for such a misdemeanour.

As time progressed, the coach and railway lines worked in unison. Where railways could not go, so the coaches expanded.

In 1890, gold was discovered in Western Australia. An enterprising gentleman bought surplus coaches, where they lay unused in Victoria, and shipped them across to start coaching lines to those gold fields. These coaches bore the name of Cobb & Co, and by 1900 W. A. Cobb & Co was flourishing.

Cobb & Co Coaches found their way to South Africa and New Zealand during their gold rush days.

Eventually the motor car and aircraft pushed the coaches off the roads. The last Cobb & Co Coach ran officially in Australia in 1924. This vehicle is now in Canberra in the National Museum.

The coach which is illustrated is reproduced by kind permission of Mr R. F. Williams. It can be seen at Bodeguero Stud, El Caballo Blanco, Wooroloo, Western Australia, where it is on loan from Mr Doug Bell of Bell Bros Transport, Western Australia. The coach is said to have been built in about 1900 and to have run on the sixty-mile road between Perth and York. It carried fourteen passengers. Those who travelled inside were protected from the weather by leather blinds. The body was made from jarrah wood and the wheels from hickory.

CONESTOGA WAGON

The Conestoga Wagon was first built in the middle of the eighteenth century and is said to take its name from its place of origin which was the Conestoga Valley, Lancaster County, Pennsylvania, USA.

It was traditionally constructed with a blue body and red under-carriage which are reputed to be the colours of Pennsylvanian folk art.

The Conestoga Wagon was used to haul freight and supplies to miners in Colorado and California during the gold rush days. The wagons were famous for their wide-rimmed wheels which were an advantage on soft ground.

The average distance covered was between ten and twenty miles a day.

Conestoga Wagon

A shorter slightly wider version, in which the family travelled, was known as the Prairie Schooner. Water was carried in barrels for the horses and oxen as they were the motive power. A small keg of water was taken in the wagon for human consumption. This was not used for washing or bathing.

The wagon illustrated here can be seen in El Pomar Carriage House Museum, Colorado Springs, Colorado, USA.

GELDERLAND COVERED WAGON (GELDERSE KLEEDWAGEN)

A dual-purpose Dutch vehicle which was used both for work on the farm and for taking the family to church on Sundays.

For farm work, it was employed as an open wagon enabling large loads to be carried if required.

When it was used as a conveyance for going to church, benches were put inside to accommodate travellers. A tilt was draped over the top to give protection against the weather.

Above: Gelderland
Covered Wagon
Left: Gypsy Wagon

On the rear of the vehicle illustrated are engraved the initials of the farmer and his wife, and the date, 1897.

It belongs to Mr W. Bakker of Vorden, Netherlands.

GYPSY WAGON

The Gypsy Wagon shown on the preceding page is thought to have been built in America in the late eighteen-hundreds.

It can be seen in the Museums at Stony Brook, New York, USA.

BURTON WAGON

The Burton Wagon probably takes its name from Burton-upon-Trent, Staffordshire, England, where the builders Orton and Spooner were well known for making this type of wagon. It is also known as a Showman's Wagon as it was used extensively by travelling showmen.

The distinguishing features of the Burton Wagon are that the rear wheels, as well as the front, are placed underneath the body and that the side walls are straighter than those of a Reading Wagon. This gives slightly more floor space.

Burton Wagon

The interior of the wagon illustrated here is carefully planned to give

maximum use to the available area. It takes a pattern which is found in many wagons though naturally each vehicle was built to suit individual requirements so there are slight variations from one to another. Mahogany and stained pine are favoured for internal wooden fittings. Amber glass handles add a finishing touch to the doors and cupboards. The wagon is entered by a front door which is divided into top and bottom halves. When the vehicle is parked and the horse is out of the shafts, the entrance is reached by curving steps.

On the right, inside the wagon, is a cupboard. Next to this is a locker seat with a chest of drawers and another seat along the wall. Across the end, below the window, is a double bed, with more sleeping space underneath which is suitable for children. On the left, at the front, is a wardrobe and cupboard. Next is the stove which is used for cooking and heating. An airing cupboard is fixed above the range. Stoves in wagons are always fitted on the offside so that the chimney pot is as far away as possible from branches of trees along the road. There is a locker seat below the window next to the fire.

The brake is of the wind-on screw-type variety. It is placed on the floor of the front porch where it can be reached by the driver of the horse or by someone walking alongside the near front wheel.

This wagon, found as a wreck, was meticulously restored by Mr Lesley Watkinson in the 1960s. With his family and the author, he drove the wagon across East Anglia when he moved house. The journey of fifty miles took three days. The average speed was about three miles an hour owing to the fact that the half-bred Percheron horse was unfit and several hills had to be negotiated for which, on occasions, a tractor had to be borrowed.

The wagon weighs over one ton.

READING WAGON

The Reading Wagon takes its name from the town of Reading in Berkshire, England, and is sometimes referred to as a Dunton Reading Wagon after the Dunton family who lived there and were noted for this type of vehicle.

The body is usually hung between tall rear wheels which were said to allow adequate room for traversing fords and similar crossings encountered on the travellers' route. The two smaller front wheels pass under the body to permit full lock. The side walls slope outwards from the floor to the roof.

Reading Wagons were considered by good Romany families to be the most favourable living accommodation of all the wagons.

The wagon which is illustrated overleaf forms part of Mrs John

Right: Reading Wagon
Below: Britzschka

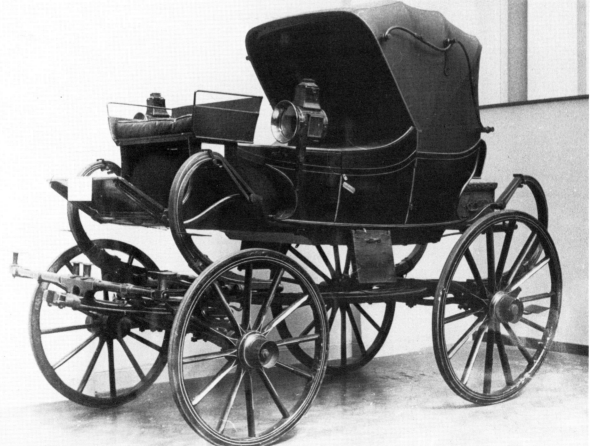

Gordon's collection at Stoke-by-Nayland, Suffolk, England, and is used as a much sought-after residence by children who visit the family.

It will be noticed that the rear wheels of this wagon lie under the body.

The Bow-Top Wagon has shallow sides and a canvas top which is fitted over a bowed wooden frame. There are no side windows so the interior is rather dark when the doors are shut. It was, however, said to be an advantage when the wagon was parked at night on or near land where the occupants preferred to remain unseen. Interior lights, shining through windows, would probably have drawn unwelcome attention to the presence of trespassers.

The Bow-Top Wagon was popular with gypsies owing to its low centre of gravity and its lightness.

It is also known as a Barrel Top Wagon, Bell, Lincolnshire, Leeds, Midland and Yorkshire Wagon.

Anyone who is in England's Cumbrian area of Appleby in June will see numerous wagons. Gypsies congregate from all over the country for the annual Appleby Fair which has taken place in this town for about seven hundred years.

BRITZSCHKA

The Britzschka was introduced to England from Austria in 1818 by Mr T. G. Adams and was used extensively as a travelling carriage in the early nineteenth century.

The vehicle accommodated four passengers when the knee flap was open and two when it was shut. Some had a glass shutter which could be let down, from the hood, filling the front and fitting tightly into a joint at the knee flap. This shutter could be conveniently stowed into a recess in the head when it was not needed. The flat bottom line of the carriage enabled long-distance travellers to lie on the floor in an attempt to sleep whilst a widespread system of postillions and post horses conveyed the occupants to their eventual destination. If postboys were not used, then the vehicle was coachman-driven from a box.

The Britzschka was often used by such people as King's Messengers in the course of their work.

Later, coachbuilders dispensed with the perch and cee-springs and built Britzschkas with elliptic springs. Some were constructed to accommodate two passengers in an open lower body. The vehicle became known as a Drosky after the Russian Driotzschka to which it was similar.

Small Britzschkas were built for use with a single horse. The leather hood had a glass front and sides which were either glazed or fitted with Venetian blinds. The door had a glass top which opened and shut independently from the lower half. The vehicle found favour as a hire carriage at seaside resorts and in country towns but was put out of work

193

by the single-horse Landau. One objection, apparently, was that difficulty was experienced in getting the glass door to operate easily as it was inclined to jam.

In order to get over pronounciation problems, the Britzschka was nicknamed a Briskie, or Brisker, by coachmen and postillions of the period. It was also known as a Briska, Britzcha, Britzska, and Britchka.

The Britzschka here was built in about 1820 and can be seen in the Transport Museum, Hull, North Humberside, England.

DORMEUSE OR EILWAGEN

The Dormeuse could be described as being the forerunner of the present-day Pullman Car. It was used as a travelling chariot in the eighteen-hundreds by such people as King's Messengers and gentry for long expeditions. The closed body was so constructed that it could be converted into sleeping accommodation for night travel. The passengers could lie flat with their feet inside the front boot. A mattress, which was carried in the boot, would be unrolled and a serviceable bed could be made with this and the cushions from the seats.

The servants travelled in a hooded dickey, which resembled a Cabriolet body.

Luggage was carried in imperials, and cap and bonnet boxes. Some

Dormeuse

Fourgon

were stowed on the roof. Others were put behind the rear seat. More boxes were packed on top of the front boot.

The carriage was hung on a perch undercarriage by cee-springs.

The vehicle was either postillion or coachman driven with either a pair or team of horses.

The Dormeuse illustrated here can be seen at Dodington Park, Chipping Sodbury, Avon, England.

The vehicle was built between 1820 and 1830 for the seventh Duke of Beaufort by Adams and Hooper. It was exhibited at South Kensington in 1873 and Crystal Palace in 1896.

FOURGON

The Fourgon was used at the turn of the century by wealthy travellers for conveying their servants and luggage. If a long journey abroad was being embarked upon, the Fourgon went ahead with clothes and other necessary items being overseen by a courier and possibly a lady's maid. They travelled in the hooded Cabriolet-type body and the luggage was stowed in numbered boxes in the van-like rear of the vehicle under a waterproof tarpaulin.

Accommodation could then be prepared and boxes unpacked in readiness for the arrival of the gentry's party who travelled independently in the family coach or similar carriage.

The Fourgon which is illustrated here can be seen in the Carriage Museum at Lancut Castle in Poland.

HANSOM CAB

The Hansom Cab first appeared in 1834 taking its name from the designer, Mr J. A. Hansom, who was an architect. The vehicle, in fact, bore little resemblance to the later Hansom Cabs which were a common sight in the streets towards the end of the last century. The original Hansom Cab looked like a large square packing case with a door on the outer side at the end of each shaft, in front of the wheels. It was driven from a seat on the front of the roof. The seven-foot-six-inch-high wheels were as tall as the roof and revolved on short stubs of axles which protruded from the body.

Modified versions of this monstrosity appeared for use as public transport but they were not a success and Mr Hansom received only a very small proportion of the £10,000 which had been promised by a company for his design.

It was Mr Chapman, the secretary of the Safety Cabriolet and Two-Wheeled Carriage Company who radically altered and greatly improved the original Hansom Cab. He sold the patent to Mr Hansom so, unfortunately, did not get full credit for his design as the original name was retained for the new cab when it appeared in 1836.

The body of the vehicle had the driver's seat at the back. It was suspended on a cranked axle. This was soon replaced by a straight axle running below the passenger's seat.

A fleet of fifty Hansom Cabs was launched and the design rapidly gained popularity. It was copied by numerous proprietors without the consent of the original company who naturally objected strongly and prosecuted the owners of these cabs. Little satisfaction was gained however so they gave up the unequal struggle. One rather ingenious gambit, which was practised by pirates, was to write the words 'Hansom's Patent Safety' on the cab preceded by a tiny 'Not' in a vain hope that this would prevent the parent company from having any grounds for prosecution.

By the 1870s, the standard of Hansom Cabs had improved enormously. The finest versions were said to have been built by Messrs Forder of London and Wolverhampton. In fact, they won a prize presented by the Society of Arts for the best two-wheeled public conveyance. The refined appearance brought about by skilled workmanship, and the reduced weight by using better materials, lighter wheels, body and under gear, resulted in a new era of street vehicles. The export trade boomed as Hansoms were in demand internationally.

Messrs Forder were the first builders to make Hansoms with doors which could be opened and shut by the driver.

Hansoms were built on a variety of springs. Some were hung on cee-springs whilst others were suspended on two side springs. Some coachbuilders favoured the use of the Dennett system with one rear cross spring and two semi-elliptic side springs.

The standards of turnout held by cab proprietors were raised when Lord Shrewsbury and Lord Lonsdale joined ranks setting a precedent with which other cab proprietors strove to compete in order to maintain their business. It was quite normal to see a Hansom Cab horsed with a high-class thoroughbred which had been passed through Tattersalls or Aldridges with the only fault that lack of speed prevented it from winning races. The animal would be immaculately turned out in a light set of highly polished harness. The cab, built by Forder, would be embellished with shining brass fittings and shod on India rubber tyres. The single door, opening against the dash, enabled easy access to the luxuriously fitted interior. There would have been rubber matting on the floor and silk blinds at the windows which might even have been decorated with an artificial flower to match the one worn by the horse on its bridle. Looking glasses, matches, ashtrays and a bell with which to communicate with the driver added to the traveller's comfort. If the cab

Hansom Cab

was one owned by Lord Shrewsbury it would have 'S' and 'T' on the outside panel meaning Earl of Shrewsbury and Talbot. Some of the coachmen were so smart that they were sometimes accused of being too dandified in appearance.

Floyd Hansoms were produced in 1885 and designed for private use. They were finished with every possible attention being paid to comfort. Some of the inside fittings were made from ivory. There were even holders specially designed to contain a stick or an umbrella and there was an interior rack for parcels. Floyd Hansoms had a hood which fitted from the front of the roof to the dash with side and front windows to allow plenty of light. This was said, however, to make the cab both cumbersome and heavy. Also there was the likelihood of broken glass and the annoyance of rattles. It was claimed that the disadvantages outweighed the advantages so these cabs never became very popular.

Victoria Cabs were similar in shape to the ordinary Hansoms but had a head which could be folded.

Court Hansoms were those on four wheels. These were not a great success.

In the late nineteenth century the cost of a Hansom Cab was between 90 and 145gns. They weighed between 8 and 10cwt and the tax payable was 15s.

Hansom Cabs were not favoured for a lady travelling alone; she would have been considered to be rather 'fast' to do so. They also had the disadvantage in that a voluminous gown could be dirtied if it brushed against a muddy wheel or apron on entering the vehicle.

Sir Walter Gilbey said, at the turn of the century, that the Hansom was an exceedingly comfortable conveyance because of its steadiness and that when the load was properly balanced no vehicle ran more easily.

The Hansom Cab was sometimes called 'The Gondola of London'.

The Hansom Cab illustrated here was built in 1978 by Croford Coachbuilders Ltd of Ashford in Kent, England, from original drawings.

BOW-FRONTED HANSOM CAB

This Hansom Cab was built in 1889 with bow-fronted doors.

It can be seen in the Transport Museum, Hull, North Humberside, England.

OPPOSITE
Above: Bow-Fronted
Hansom Cab
Below: Reversed-Seat
Leisure Carriage

REVERSED-SEAT LEISURE CARRIAGE

This unusual carriage was built by Binder of Paris in about 1900.

The vehicle is in the Lancut Castle Museum in Poland. It is thought

that it could have been a present from Roman Potocki, the third master of Lancut, to his wife Elzbieta Radziwill.

The carriage is constructed to seat two passengers in the rear backward-facing body. They are fully protected from the weather by a folding hood and wooden apron.

Various theories are suggested about the reason for the rare design of this carriage. One is that when the hood was lowered, the passengers could enjoy an unobstructed view of the countryside. Another is that the smell of horse was avoided. Perhaps it was originally built for someone who was allergic to horses but had to travel considerable distances.

Whatever the reason, the vehicle turned out to be impractical because when the roads were dry the interior became extremely dusty and unpleasant.

BROUGHAM

The Brougham (pronounced broo-em) was first introduced to England in 1838 when it was built to a design by Lord Brougham by Messrs Robinson and Cook of London. Lord Brougham felt that there was need for 'a refined and glorified street cab which would make a convenient carriage for a gentleman, and especially for a man of such ideas as one who carried his own carpet bag on occasions when time was important and his own servants otherwise employed'. There was a distinct need for a light cab which could be drawn by a single horse for city use. Lord Brougham took his plans to his coachbuilders, Messrs Sharp and Bland of South Audley Street, London. Accustomed as they were to building such family conveyances of grandeur as Barouches and Landaus, they rejected the idea as unsuitable. So Lord Brougham took his business to a neighbouring firm who were delighted to be given the commission.

Lord Brougham's original vehicle was completed on 15th May 1838. The olive-green body was fitted with a sword case. Weapons had been carried in case protection was needed during the early days of long-distance travel. This fixture was a relic from that period and was omitted from later Broughams. An opera board was fitted to the rear of the body. This was to protect travellers' backs from the possibility of the pole of a following vehicle piercing the rear of the carriage and injuring the occupants during peak period travel in crowded London streets. The body was hung on five springs behind and two full elliptic springs in front. The carriage was heavily plated throughout to hold it together. Iron stays connected the front pillars to the front boot by means of bolts.

In 1840 this original Brougham was sold to Sir William Foulis as it had been replaced by an improved version which had been completed in 1839. It then went to Lord Henry Bentinck and then was passed on to Earl Bathurst. Such statesmen as Lord Beaconsfield, Disraeli and

Gladstone are said to have used it. The Brougham which is illustrated here can now be seen in the Science Museum in London.

It was not long before Broughams were being built by coachbuilders throughout the country. Many varieties emerged as craftsmen altered and improved upon the original design. Some were built with bow fronts and curving windows so that three people could be accommodated. Others were made with vis-à-vis seating for four and became known as double Broughams.

Messrs G. Hooper & Co made the first cee-spring Brougham in 1845 for the Earl of Belfast.

In 1850 Mr Edward Lytton Bulwer, who later became Lord Lytton, had a rather dressy version built. It was painted brown with white wheels and had a brown and white hammercloth on the box and a rear platform for footmen.

In 1885 Messrs Holmes of Derby sent to the Inventions Exhibition a single Brougham which had a leather roof instead of a wooden one. Ventilation slots between the roof and the lining allowed air to flow through, which lessened the drumming noise previously experienced. Mulliner exhibited a Brougham at the same venue which was hung on Tilbury springs.

Sir Walter Gilbey, at the turn of the century, ordered a Brougham designed by Shanks for use with a postillion pair because he objected to the front window being blocked by the coachman's box seat. He also

Brougham

devised a ventilation system to allow tobacco smoke to escape without a draught being caused 'to ensure purity of the atmosphere within the Brougham when the weather obliges it to be closed'.

Interiors of many Broughams were fitted out luxuriously with appliances to make travellers' journeys more comfortable. A reading lamp, looking glass, card pocket and clock were some of the accessories which came with a de-luxe version.

A luggage basket was frequently put onto the roof so that cases could be carried. This was taken off if the Brougham was being used for such occasions as a visit to the theatre or an outing to dinner.

Speaking tubes enabled passengers to give orders to the coachman.

It was quite usual to keep two sets of wheels. Ones with rubber tyres were used for London's wooden paving and others with iron tyres would be fitted for macadamised country roads. Collinge's axles simplified the oiling of wheels when the job was quickly done by removing, filling and replacing the oil in the caps on the hubs.

In the late eighteen-hundreds, the tax payable for a small single Brougham was one guinea a year and double that for a heavy carriage of this type constructed to take a pair.

The cost, in the latter quarter of the century, of having a single Brougham built was in the region of 150gns whereas a double version would have cost up to 190gns and a larger, pair-horse Brougham up to 240gns.

A single Brougham could be hired from a jobmaster at the end of the nineteenth century for about £222 a year, providing that the hirer kept within seven miles of Charing Cross. The jobmaster would supply a Brougham which was painted as desired and turned out to a high standard. He also provided the horse, which would be replaced if it became unfit for work, as well as its food and shoes, the harness and the liveried coachman who, incidentally, could not be regarded as the hirer's servant. This matter apparently caused some inconvenience at times.

If it was just the vehicle which was required then it could be hired for about £40 a year with the Brougham becoming the property of the hirer after five years if the contract had been so agreed.

Broughams found great favour amongst the medical profession when they affectionately became known as 'Pill Boxes'.

Of all the carriage builders, none were said to have equalled Messrs Barker for the production of Broughams.

Broughams can be seen in numerous museums throughout Britain and a few are still employed in some towns.

They are used daily from the Royal Mews, London, to convey The Queen's official dispatch boxes to ministries in the city.

ROTHMAN'S BROUGHAM

Rothman's Brougham

Rothman's of Pall Mall turn out an immaculate Brougham which was built in 1867. It is finished in red and gold with twenty-one coats of hand-applied paint. The original curtains and brocades still exist inside. The handles are of silver and ivory. The coachmen wear uniforms of fawn with red trim whilst driving a grey pair to execute deliveries in London covering about seventy miles a week. Rothman's are said to be the only tobacco company in the world who still deliver cigarettes in this manner.

The equipage is a big winner in trade classes at shows throughout the country.

The horses and carriage are now housed at Elvaston Mews near Queen's Gate, London, SW7.

CLARENCE

In 1842 a carriage which was halfway between a Brougham and a coach was designed and built by Laurie and Marner of Oxford Street, London. This became known as a Clarence.

Clarence

Most Clarences are square fronted but there is, at Balmoral Castle, one with a curved front which was made by Clarke of Aberdeen, Scotland.

The Clarence seats four passengers and was driven by a coachman from a low box for town work with a pair of horses.

Clarence cabs were used by cabmen plying for hire in the middle of the nineteenth century. They were drawn by a single horse and considered to be more dignified than a Hansom Cab. Also, there was more room for luggage as it could be stowed on the roof.

The Clarence cab was sometimes referred to as a Growler owing to the noise which was made by its progress.

This vehicle can be seen in connection with the Science Museum, London, England.

GLASS-PANEL ROCKAWAY

OPPOSITE
Above: Glass-Panel
Rockaway
Below: Char-de-Côté

The Rockaway is an American vehicle. The first of its type is reputed to have been built in about 1830 in Jamaica, Long Island, New York.

The Rockaway was used for town and country activities and was both

owner and coachman driven. The body is usually hung on two elliptic springs. on a central perch. The arch permits half lock.

The vehicle illustrated here was built in about 1900 by Studebaker and can be seen in the Museums at Stony Brook, Long Island, New York, to whom it was presented by Mr and Mrs Ward Melville in 1971.

CHAR-DE-CÔTÉ

This eighteenth-/nineteenth-century carriage was designed for use in Switzerland. Its seats faced the side of the road, enabling travellers to look at the beautiful views whilst they were going along. This must have been preferable to the dull view of the coachman's back which was offered with so many carriages.

The vehicle can be seen in the Swiss Transport Museum in Lucerne, Switzerland.

BAROUCHE

The Barouche had been seen in England by 1767. It was, to begin with, a somewhat cumbersome vehicle. The body was said to be so low that no mounting step for passengers was necessary. The box seat is described as being placed well forward over the horses and the footman is recorded to have stood on a platform at the rear of the vehicle.

By 1808, the Barouche was being used by members of the Four-Horse Club, also known as the Barouche Club, Whip Club and Four-in-Hand Club. This Club was founded by Mr Charles Buxton, originator of the Buxton bit, when gentlemen Whips drove their Barouches, in preference to Drags, on Club outings for dinner and similar occasions. Club rules stipulated that the Barouches should be yellow bodied, with 'dickies', drawn by bay horses wearing silver-mounted harness with rosettes on their bridles. Apparently though, one member is reported to have driven greys and another roans so the rule was obviously not strictly enforced. It is fortunate for twentieth-century carriage driving enthusiasts that present-day clubs throughout the world do not lay down such stringent rules.

Sir John Lade is said to have tooled his Barouche with a team of six horses, from the Brighton Pavilion to Lewes Races where the vehicle acted ably as a grandstand for Sir John and his guests. This carriage has been referred to as a German Waggon.

In 1810 a Barouche was built at the time of Napoleon's wedding by a Milan craftsman. The vehicle had two well-shaped solid iron perches, and was hung on cee-springs.

In 1816 there was a Barouche designed by Ackerman which was

suspended between high wheels by whip springs.

Gradually, Barouches with deep panels on wooden perches gave way to lighter vehicles with shallower canoe-shaped bodies which were hung from leather braces on cee-springs on single iron perches. The coachman's seat was built on curved irons.

Some were constructed so much on the lines of Landaus that they were known as Barouche Landaus. Smaller editions were described as Barouchets.

In its heyday the Barouche was used extensively as a summer vehicle for park driving. The rear hooded seat had a leather apron which could be drawn up to elbow height to give protection to travellers. When this knee flap was in use the rear-facing front seat was put out of action.

The Barouche was considered to be one of the most fashionable of the larger carriages, requiring pairs of high quality horses, with substance, in order that it could be turned out to the desired standard. Messrs Hooper, who were noted for their Barouches, claimed that by the last quarter of the nineteenth century the depression of agriculture had seriously affected the coachbuilding trade in general and that of Barouches in particular. Financial problems were preventing many people from being able to afford the luxury of such an equipage and single-horse vehicles, like Victorias, were taking their place.

However, at the turn of the century, there were reports that the Barouche was once more gaining favour.

Barouche

At the end of the century a Barouche on cee- and under-springs would have cost between 180gns and 280gns to buy from a London coachbuilder and 2gns a year to tax. The weight of the vehicle was between 13 and 17 cwt.

A Barouche on elliptic springs weighed between 11 and 13 cwt and cost between 100 and 200gns to buy.

Illustrated here is a Barouche at the Royal Mews, Buckingham Palace, London, which is frequently used on such ceremonial occasions as the Trooping of the Colour. This carriage can be seen on open days when the general public is allowed to view the contents of the coach-houses and harness rooms.

SOCIABLE

According to the coachbuilder William Felton, in the eighteenth century, the Sociable gained its name owing to the fact that a number of people could be accommodated at one time for family excursions. He also recommended that it was ideal for a gentleman's use in the park. Felton said too that the Sociable was a convenient carriage for transporting the servants from one residence to another.

The Sociable was owner driven from a box at the front and had a seat which backed onto that of the driver's. Protection against the weather, in Felton's Sociable, was given to travellers on these seats by a jointed umbrella which served all four people. The rear of the vehicle resembled a hooded gig on whip springs. A sword case was fitted at the back. The body was entered by folding steps. A knee flap, which buttoned at elbow height, could be fastened to cover the space between the vis-à-vis seats.

The undercarriage was built with a crane neck perch to allow full lock. The straked wheels had ten spokes in front and twelve behind.

Felton designed the body so that it could be placed onto the carriage (undercarriage) of a chariot or coach thus saving the expense of two complete vehicles though in the 1820s the annual tax of £3 was payable for each additional body.

The cost of a Sociable built by Felton in about 1890, was in the region of £101 10s.

Later Sociables, of the mid-eighteen-hundreds, were similar in many ways to Felton's earliest editions though they were coachman driven with the box seat higher than the passenger seats. There was a door on each side of the body. The perch undercarriage gave way to four elliptic springs.

It was usual to horse a Sociable with a pair. By the end of the eighteen-hundreds, ladies were using the Sociable as a summer vehicle for park driving.

Vehicles which were similar to the Sociable gradually gained favour. The Barouche Sociable was built with a double-hooded body. The

Sociable Landau was built on the lines of a Landau with a low box on which were seated a coachman and footman. It was considered that the vehicle was a compromise between a Dress Landau for dignity and a Sociable for suspension and discreet finish. Its angular body seated four passengers and the hind seat had a folding head. This vehicle would have probably been used for smart town work when an eye-catching pair would have been put to, to impress those who mattered.

The Sociable illustrated here was built by the famous London coachbuilders, Peters and Company. It formed a part of the late Robert Kaye's collection.

VICTORIA

The Victoria was a coachman-driven vehicle which became fashionable in the latter half of the eighteen-hundreds, as a result of its popularity with Queen Victoria when she was still Princess.

Opinions vary regarding the origin of the Victoria. Some authorities claim that it was first built by an English coachbuilder whilst others say that it owed its ancestry to a Continental vehicle.

The low entry, comfortable and hooded seating, and curved splash boards which protected the passengers' clothes, combined with the elegant profile, made the Victoria a suitable conveyance for ladies wishing to be taken on shopping trips or paying afternoon calls during the summer months.

Victorias were built to numerous designs. Some were open with vis-à-vis seating to accommodate four travellers. Some had low doors at the sides. Many were constructed to be drawn by a single horse. Others were made for pairs of ponies or horses.

Victorias are not correct for private driving showing classes or for combined driving events as they are essentially 'coachman-driven vehicles'. They are, however, sought after as wedding carriages and sightseeing vehicles for which purposes they are extremely suitable.

The Victoria which is illustrated here was built in 1900 and forms part of Mrs John Friend's collection in Wisconsin, USA. It is hung on cee-springs. The skeleton box seat is removable so that the carriage can be postillion driven.

DRESS LANDAU

This Dress Landau, which dates from about 1698, was owned by the Baskerville family of Clyro in Powys, Wales. It is said to be one of the earliest existing British-made carriages in England.

The Landau stood for about twenty-five years from 1898 in Fullers Coach & Harness Manufacturers' showroom in Bath on loan from Dr. J. Blake Maurice who then owned the vehicle.

Fortunately, it then went to the Nottingham Castle Museum where it was saved from destruction as Fullers' works were demolished by incendiary bombs in World War II.

This carriage will be on view in the Industrial Museum, Wollaton Park, Nottingham, England, when restoration has been completed.

LANDAU

The Landau originated in the West German fortified town of Landau. Early Landaus were heavy vehicles, built on a substantial perch undercarriage and hung by leather braces on whip or cee-springs. The hoods only opened halfway, lying at an angle of about 45 degrees and were said to be extremely disagreeable. They needed constant applications of blacking and oil to keep the leather soft and the unpleasant feel and odour was considerable.

In 1838, a London coachbuilder, Luke Hopkinson, with great foresight, produced a vehicle which he called a Britzka Landau. The seats

OPPOSITE
Above: Victoria
Below: Dress Landau

210

of the carriage were raised and the hoods made to lie nearly flat which gave the passengers more room and a comfortable ride.

The Landau gained popularity owing to the fact that it combined the qualities of a Brougham and a Victoria. The perfect arrangement was, of course, to have both of those carriages so that the Brougham was available for rainy days and the Victoria for sunny conditions. If economy was necessary then a Landau could be used to combine the roles of a summer and winter carriage. When the heads were raised winter protection could be given to the four vis-à-vis travellers whilst hoods could be folded down, on a fine day, to convert the carriage into an open conveyance allowing passengers to take the air. Costs were considerably cut as only one vehicle had to be housed, maintained and taxed. The latter, in 1888, was £2 2s 0d per annum. Also, the lighter editions needed only a single horse as the motive power.

Coachmakers throughout the country quickly put their ideas into practice to improve the Landau.

By halfway through the eighteen-hundreds efforts were being made to reduce the weight and many builders dispensed with the perch. Elliptic springs were used in front and either five springs (one cross, two elbow and two side) or elliptic springs were used at the rear.

The head was improved to such an extent that it was said to be as easy to open and shut as an umbrella or parasol.

Step covers were designed which opened with the carriage door to reveal a clean surface by which the passengers could mount and dismount.

Joints on the roof were perfected, with weather plates, to keep out the rain.

The iron body plates, which were used to stiffen the carriage, were replaced by mild steel which helped to reduce the weight.

It was claimed at the approach of the last quarter of the eighteen-hundreds that no vehicle had had, in twenty years, so much inventive talent, care and attention from designers and coachbuilders as the Landau.

At the end of the century a Shelburne or Sefton Landau was said to weigh between 11 and 15 cwt and cost between 180gns and 250gns to buy.

The Sefton Landau was first built by Messrs Hooper for the Earl of Sefton and exhibited at the Inventions Exhibition in 1885. It had a canoe-shaped lower outline, similar to that of a Barouche. It was lighter than its predecessors and suitable for a single horse. The cost and difficulty of obtaining pairs of good carriage horses made people consider the use of a single-horse vehicle. One trade journal contributor apparently found it incredible that a vehicle of such aristocratic parentage as a Landau should sink to the depths of being exhibited as suitable for a single animal.

Shelburne Landaus, named after the first of this type which was built for the Earl of Shelburne, had a square profile with a well for the feet. The silhouette, in many ways, resembled a Sociable.

Landaus could be drawn by a team of postillion- or coachman-driven horses.

The Landau Grande Daumont is not a particular type of Landau but refers to a postillion-driven Landau with similarly dressed out-riders on comparable horses, wearing matching bridles and cruppers, flanking the equipage. The term takes its name from the Duc d'Aumont.

State Landaus from the Royal Mews, Buckingham Palace, London, are used for such occasions as the Royal procession for the State Opening of Parliament when these magnificent carriages are turned out lavishly. Lighter, postillion-driven, Ascot Landaus with basketwork sides may be seen when the Queen drives up the course at the Royal Ascot race meeting.

Landaus are not suitable for either combined driving events or private driving classes as they are coachman-driven vehicles. They are used extensively for conveying trippers at seaside resorts on sightseeing tours. They are also popular for weddings, when the bride and groom can travel from the church to the reception in an open carriage with the comforting thought that the hoods can be raised should it rain.

The State Landau illustrated here can be viewed at the Royal Mews in London on certain days when the carriage houses are open to the public.

Landau

SEFTON LANDAU

OPPOSITE
Above : Sefton Landau
Below : Five-Glass
Landau

This Sefton Landau was built by Atkinson and Philipson of Newcastle. It formed part of the late Robert Kaye's collection.

FIVE-GLASS LANDAU

The name Five-Glass Landau refers to the extra three windows. Most Landaus were built with two hoods and central glasses which pulled up between the hoods from the doors. The three windows at the front of this vehicle give more light, when the hood is up, than the more conventional arrangement which is found with most Landaus.

This vehicle was built by Brewster & Co, New York, USA, in 1890, and belongs to Mrs John Friend of Wisconsin.

It is fitted with both whipple trees and a splinter bar, for a pair, so that either breast collars or full collars can be used on the horses.

LISTER CHAISE

The Lister Chaise is said to be one of the oldest carriages in England, being built in the early seventeen-hundreds for James Lister of Shibden in Yorkshire.

Lister Chaise

The vehicle is hung on whip springs from a perch undercarriage. The steps, by which the passengers entered the carriage, are designed to fold. The footman travelled on a platform between the rear springs, holding on by means of straps at the back of the body.

The wheels, which are heavily dished, are straked (i.e. strips of iron cover the joints between the felloes) instead of each wheel being shod with a continuous iron band as was the later practice. A splinter-bar stay connects the end of the axle to the end of the splinter bar.

The carriage was postillion driven in an unusual way. The offside horse was harnessed between shafts and the ridden, nearside horse was in just traces. The problems encountered in slowing down and stopping must have been considerable in that the ridden horse could have been hit in the hind legs by the front of the carriage if the shaft horse kept going.

There is a brake hook, suspended from the underneath of the carriage by a chain, which was fixed round one wheel when a hill had to be negotiated.

The vehicle can be seen at Shibden Hall, Halifax, Yorkshire.

The illustration is reproduced by kind permission of the Calderdale Museums Service.

FAMILY CHARIOT (TRAVELLING CHARIOT)

This type of chariot was used extensively in the nineteenth century by families for travelling.

The body, which seated two people inside, was hung on cee-springs. A sword case was fitted to the back so that weapons could be carried. Leather straps connected the body to the perch to prevent excessive side sway.

The pair or team was either driven from the box seat or ridden by postillions. There was accommodation at the rear for servants.

The carriage which is illustrated here was owned, at one time, by the Baskerville family of Clyro in Powys, Wales. It can be seen in the Industrial Museum, Wollaton Park, Nottingham, England.

STATE CHARIOT

The State Chariot reached the peak of its perfection at the time of Queen Victoria's coronation. It was essentially a carriage for state and court occasions, used mainly by noblemen, when strict formality was desirable.

The State Chariot, like all chariots, seated two people, facing forward.

Family Chariot

The body, which was made of mahogany, was hung on cee-springs from a carved and gilded perch undercarriage. The carriage was finished in the family colours; crests and arms embellished the quarters and doors. The coachman's seat was covered with an ornate, heavily tasselled hammercloth. The family arms were embroidered in silk or metal to match the design on the doors. Wilton carpeting was used to trim the interior of the chariot and blinds adorned the windows. The metal work on the door handles and lamps was ornate and in keeping with the furniture on the harness. Travellers who wished to look along the road through the front window of the chariot had the coachman's seat removed and travelled behind a postillion-driven pair or team.

The coachman and footmen of a State Chariot wore state livery comprising of knee breeches, stockings, buckled shoes and corded livery coats of velvet or coloured material. All wore white wigs. The coachman had a three-cornered hat. The two footmen, who wore cocked hats, stood on a platform between the cee-springs at the back of the chariot, hanging on by means of holders made from tassels and braid.

The fact that so many State Chariots still exist is proof of the high quality of workmanship which was bestowed upon them.

The State Chariot illustrated overleaf was built in about 1890 for the

State Chariot

twentieth Earl of Shrewsbury and was used on the state visit to Ireland in 1911 and at the coronations of Edward VII and Elizabeth II. It can be seen in the Museum of Staffordshire Life, Shugborough, England.

THE PROCESSIONAL CHARIOT OF OUR LADY OF CABO

The ornate carriage illustrated here was built in about 1740. The body is hung on leather braces. Check braces are fixed between the body and the perch to lessen the sideways sway.

The chariot was pulled by four mules, driven by postillions. Four footservants walked alongside the carriage, carrying lighted torches.

The vehicle can be seen in the National Coach Museum in Lisbon.

BUGATTI COACH

OPPOSITE
Above: Processional Chariot
Below: Bugatti Coach

This vehicle, which has a chariot-type body, was one of reputedly four carriages to be built by Ettore Bugatti (1881–1947) who was more famous for his cars.

218

The carriage is finished in his personal colours of black and yellow. (Bugatti cars were raced in the well-known 'Bugatti blue' but Ettore retained black and yellow for his own use wherever possible.) There is, for some unexplained reason, a design error in the carriage in that when the wheels are turned to full lock, it is not possible to open the door.

It is said that Bugatti planned to drive the vehicle over the Alps from Strasbourg to his birth place in Milan. However, this did not materialize as in 1936 Bugatti left Molshein during the industrial troubles.

In 1940 the coach went to Ermenonville, a chateau which Bugatti had bought from Prince Radziwill, where it remained during World War II.

Later, Baron Casier was approached by Lidea Bugatti, the Countess of Boigne, to take over the carriages belonging to Bugatti. He has completed the upholstery and restored the vehicle to perfection; it is now in his collection in Belgium.

LUCY COACH
(see colour illustration facing page 177)

This travelling coach was the main carriage used by George and Mary Elizabeth Lucy who, with their six children aged between six months and ten years, journeyed from England to Southern Italy and back over a period of twenty months between 1841 and 1843.

The coach was drawn by a postillion-driven team of four horses.

The body is hung on cee-springs. Straps to the perch from the body prevented too much sideways sway.

The mounting steps folded so that they were kept free from mud.

The drag shoe can clearly be seen hanging from the hook on the perch. This was applied under a rear wheel at the top of steep hills as no brakes were used.

The Lucy Coach can be seen at Charlecote Park in Warwickshire, England.

The Lucy pike (the fish, not the weapon), part of the family coat of arms, decorates the lavishly upholstered interior of the coach.

BERLIN

This nineteenth-century Berlin is hung by cee-springs onto a crane-neck perch undercarriage.

It is coachman driven from a box seat which is adorned with an ornate hammercloth.

It can be seen in the National Museum at Versailles in France.

The carriage is a Berlin of the first empire. It was restored for the christening of the Duke of Bordeaux and afterwards for the wedding of Napoleon III.

Berlin

KING JOHN V's COACH

The ornately carved and decorated state coach seen overleaf was built in Lisbon in about 1725.

It is considered to be the best carriage in the collection in the National Coach Museum in Lisbon, Portugal, regarding the technical and artistic work.

The carving is thought to have been executed by two foremost Portuguese sculptors, José de Almeida and his brother Felix Vicente de Almeida.

The rear wheels are decorated with carvings showing the signs of the zodiac.

The paintings on the panels are attributed to Pierre Antoine Quillard.

The roof is covered in red velvet and embroidered with silver threads. The carriage is decorated with gilt bronze handles and ornamental studs.

King John V's Coach

The coach has been used by numerous heads of foreign states including the Emperors of Brazil (Pedro II) and Germany (Kaiser Wilhelm V) and by King Oscar of Sweden, Edward VII of England, Alfonso XIII of Spain, and by the French President Emile Loubet.

STATE COACH

This 1825 carriage of King Charles X was refurbished for the christening of the Prince Imperial, son of Napoleon III, in 1856.

It can be seen in the National Museum at Versailles in France.

TRIUMPHAL COACH

This coach, which can be seen in the National Coach Museum in Lisbon, Portugal, is famous for the lavishly sculptured decorations with the allegorical group at the rear. It shows a woman symbolizing Lisbon (capital of the Portuguese Empire), crowned by a symbol of Fame, with 'Abundance' at her right and 'Africa' and 'Asia' near her feet.

Above: State Coach
Left: Triumphal Coach

223

The coach was ordered in Rome, Italy, by King John V and sent to Pope Clement XI in 1716.

The vehicle is thought to have been made by Portuguese students who were studying in Rome at that time, being financed by the Portuguese king.

GOLD STATE COACH

(see also colour illustration facing page 177)

The Gold State Coach, which was delivered to the Royal Mews at 5 am on 24th November 1762, was said to be one of the most remarkable examples of carriage building that had ever been seen.

The coach is twelve feet high, twenty-four feet long and eight feet three inches wide. The pole adds a further twelve feet four inches to the length. The overall weight is four tons.

The gilded and elaborately carved body is hung from four tritons (sea-nymphs) by four morocco leather braces, decorated with ornate gilt buckles. Those at the front of the coach announce the approach of the Monarch of the Ocean through conch shells, used as trumpets, as they appear to draw the coach by cables which are attached to cranes passing over their shoulders. The tritons at the rear of the coach carry the Imperial fasces with tridents at the top. The coach body is framed by eight carved palm trees. There is one on each side of the central door. Four more, at the corners, emerge from the backs of the heads of lions and are designed to show the symbols of victory relating to the Seven Years War which had recently ended when the coach was built. The palm leaves branch at the roof to form a surround. Three cherubs are standing in the centre of the roof to represent the genii of England, Scotland and Ireland. They are supporting the royal crown and are holding the sceptre, the sword of state and the ensign of knighthood. Laurel leaves are draped from their bodies to the corners by the palms.

The body panels were painted by Giovanni Battista Cipriani who came to England from Italy in 1755.

The coachman's footboard is designed like a large scallop shell and decorated with water plants of varying types.

The splinter bar has a dolphin's head at each end of the rich moulding.

The wheels are fastidiously carved and resemble those of an ancient triumphal car.

The pole is designed to give the appearance of a bundle of lances.

The coach was driven round the Mews on that first morning in 1762, at 8 am, with eight cream horses. It was, no doubt, a great relief to Sir William Chambers, an architect and surveyor to His Majesty's Board of Works, who had selected the designs for the vehicle, that the coach was found to be satisfactory.

The next day, King George III drove in the coach to open Parliament. Crowds turned out to admire the magnificent carriage and it was later recorded that: 'the new State Coach was the most superb and expensive of any ever built in this kingdom'.

Since George IV, the coach has been used for every coronation and it was frequently employed by the sovereign for the occasion of the opening of a new session of Parliament. After World War II it had been used only for The Queen's coronation in 1953, until 1977 when it was horsed with eight greys, wearing state harness, ridden by postillions in state livery, for Her Majesty The Queen's Silver Jubilee procession.

Originally, the vehicle was driven from the box with the coachman handling six of the horses and a postillion managing the two leaders. Then King Edward VII claimed that the hammercloth and coachman prevented people from seeing Queen Alexandra and himself and he had the box seat removed.

Until World War I the coach was drawn by a team of eight cream stallions. Then, in 1921 and 1922, black horses were used. From 1923 until King George VI's coronation bay horses pulled the coach. Since then, greys have been favoured.

The coach was built by a carriage maker called Butler, carved by Wilton and gilded by Pajolas.

The cost of producing the coach was £7,652 16s 9½d of which:

£2,500 0s 0d went to the carver

£1,763 15s 6d went to the coachmaker

£933 14s 0d went to the gilder

£737 10s 7d went to the lacemaker

£666 4s 6d went to the chaser

£385 15s 0d went to the harnessmaker

£315 0s 0d went to the painter

£202 5s 10½d went to the mercer

£99 9s 6d went to the bitmaker

£31 3s 4d went to the milliner

£10 6s 6d went to the saddler

£4 2s 6d went to the woollen draper

£3 9s 6d went to the covermaker

These figures were after between £300 and £400 had been taken off for tax.

The coach can be seen at the Royal Mews, Buckingham Palace, London, on days when the coach-houses are open to the public.

OVERLEAF
Gold State Coach

226

227

PRESERVATION OF CARRIAGES

by William Bridges Adams (1837)

'The materials of a carriage are as delicate, and require as much care, as the furniture of a drawingroom; and therefore they should be as carefully preserved from stable contact as the satin couches of the drawingroom. After the carriage has been out, whether in the sun or the rain, it should be carefully washed, and, above all, dried, taking care to wet the leather as little as possible during the operation. It is a common practice to wash the carriage, and then leave the water to drip away. After drying, the leather and especially the braces, should be slightly rubbed with an oily rag to restore all that had been consumed in the day; and the carriage should then be placed to stand in a dry well-ventilated apartment with a boarded floor, leaving a clear passage for the air beneath it, and, if at all convenient, having warm air passing through to ensure its dryness. Above all, it should be away from all stables, dung-heaps, cesspools, or open drains. A gentleman should avoid placing his carriage in any situation where he would not wish to place his wardrobe; and with regard to the interior lining, he should treat it much in the same manner. If the carriage be laid by for a time, it should occasionally be brushed out, and have a current of warm air passed through it. Cedar shavings should also be placed in it. If an open carriage, it will require more care than a close one. The hammercloth should be covered with the waterproof India rubber material, and cedar shavings should be interposed between them. The blacking should also be washed off the leather work, and a composition of oil and tallow rubbed into it to preserve it. The iron-work should be kept painted wherever it may have been chipped, and the whole of the woodwork, and especially the wheels, frequently washed over with water – this more particularly in the summer time. The metalwork should be cleaned occasionally with whitening or platepowder, and rubbed every day with a soft leather; it will thus last much longer than when it is suffered to tarnish frequently. If common axles, they should never be suffered to run more than seventy or eighty miles without fresh greasing. If mail axles, they should be looked to when new every three weeks; – if old, every week. If the patent oil axles, they will run between three and four thousand miles without fresh oiling; and when this is done, it is better to send for the carriagebuilder or engineer to do it, if practicable, than to trust to a servant, unless he has been previously well instructed in it. The wheel-plate will also require occasional greasing, and a new leather will be required to the transom. The suspending braces should also be carefully watched, as they are apt to cut and strain at the eyes and angles. A carriage carefully attended to in this manner will yield one third more service than one which is neglected.'

Part VI
CARRIAGES OF THE LATE TWENTIETH CENTURY

TANDEM GIG

The vehicle illustrated here is Mr and Mrs Biff Riley's Tandem Gig which is seen regularly at Meets of The Tandem Club of Great Britain.

At the begining of the 1970s, very few people were driving a tandem, and it was feared, by the small number of enthusiasts who were practising the art, that the skills might become lost for ever. In 1975, at Lowther, the author became the first person to complete a Three-Day Driving Trial with a tandem. Soon after that, Mr Richard James, an accomplished tandem Whip, suggested that a Tandem Club might be formed.

In 1977, Lady Cromwell, also a keen tandem driver, offered to host the first Meet and drive from her home in Oxfordshire, and The Tandem Club of Great Britain was founded. The author has since arranged for hosts to organise annual Meets in different parts of the country. This has enabled tandem drivers from all over Great Britain, and a few visitors from overseas, to become members and gain their silver 'tandem bar' badge. By 1991, 137 Whips, including Mr Riley, had qualified for their 'bars' by driving at an annual Meet. Tandem Clubs are also flourishing in the U.S.A. and New Zealand, and the demand for tandem vehicles has increased.

This Tandem Gig has the unusual claim of being constructed by two coach-builders, for Mr Riley of Scunthorpe, England. Mr Riley's interest in tandem driving with his Welsh ponies, Brynmair Cardi and Brynmair Fury, resulted in a desire for a tandem vehicle. The original vehicle was built, in 1984, by Mr C. J. Nicholson and painted by the late Mr John Ousbey. In 1985, a new body was built by Mr John Ousbey for the original carriage.

The idea for the design was based on the Tandem Gig which is illustrated in Francis Underhill's book *Driving for Pleasure* published in 1897. Mr Underhill states that this design is one of several which 'have been adopted as standard by The Tandem Club of New York'. The vehicles were, in the main, copies of carriages seen in

old sporting prints. This particular design was said to have been taken from the picture by H. Alken Sen., 1823, of *A Sporting Tandem* and thought, by Underhill, 'to be a very good pattern of a tandem vehicle to carry two'.

The body shape has a distinct concave curve in the rear panel which gives it a sporting flavour. The ash shafts run under the black body to add to the height. The red wooden wheels run on axles of the Collinge pattern but also have modern roller bearings. The Gig is finished with about sixteen layers of paint.

HAREWOOD SPORTING GIG

This Harewood Sporting Gig was built for the author by The Harewood Carriage Company. The triangular-profiled body has a fixed seat which accommodates the driver and one passenger. The rear panel lets down to give access to the large boot allowing plenty of storage space for headcollar, rugs, picnic, spares etc.

The body of the vehicle is decorated with cane panels which are glued onto the wooden structure. The dash and splash boards are covered with leather. The metal wheels rotate on roller bearings and are secured by a central bolt which is tightened by an Allen key. One feature, which is of particular interest, is that the wooden shafts can be altered for length and height so that this vehicle can be used for animals ranging from 13.2 h.h. to 14.3 h.h. The operation of changing the shafts, which are fixed by bolts to the front and rear of the body, can be achieved by anyone who has a Tommy Bar for the round-headed bolts at the front, and a spanner for the rear bolts. The slope on the receiving slots results in the shafts being lengthened when they are heightened and vice versa.

Harewood Sporting Gig

Close-up view of shaft
fixings at front of body of
Harewood Sporting Gig

STICK-BACK GIG

Stick-Back Gig

This Gig was built by Mr Nick Wood of Fairbourne Carriages in Kent, England, on a traditional design using his own plans. The body has an ash frame with mahogany panels and is hung on Dennett springs. The splash and dash boards are covered with patent leather, and the shafts are of laminated ash. Draught is taken through a swingletree on leather-covered chains which go down to the axle. The wooden wheels run on original Collinge axles which have come from Fairbourne Carriages' store.

CEE-SPRING STICK-BACK GIG

This Gig was made to measure by Keith and Grace Randall of Hampshire, England, for Mr and Mrs Brian Wood and their daughter Sarah Louise. Various sketches were drawn, by the Randalls, to comply with the family's requirements. The Woods eventually chose the design which best suited Sarah Louise's purposes for showing her Welsh pony in private driving classes.

Sarah Louise and the pony were measured so that the vehicle would fit both when it was finally completed. Scale drawings were then made so that everyone could be satisfied that they liked the proportions and appearance of the Gig. These drawings were then transferred, in full size, with the minimum of lines, onto a sheet of hardboard, allowing front, back and side views, for further approval.

Patterns were made for the springsmith to make the cee springs. The body was made with an ash frame and top quality mahogany marine ply; this was used in preference to solid boards to avoid wide-area splits occurring. The top rail, above the spindles, was laminated. The spindles were turned in hornbeam for strength. The body was then assembled, with a few screws, so that it could be tried for size and balance. Once approved, the body was dismantled. Pillars were reeded and surfaces were domed in order to reflect light once the Gig had been painted. The wheels were assembled with cleaved-oak spokes and ash felloes on an elm hub. An old axle box and stub axles, dated 1901, were used. The ironwork fittings were made by Randall Carriages and sent away for specialist welding, and the welds were hand filed to give a traditional appearance. The shafts were made of laminated ash.

The Gig was put together once more for a final fitting and a check for balance. The leather upholstery was made by Grace Randall. The carriage was then taken apart, yet again, for painting with numerous coats of traditional paint before the final assembly. More paint, lining and varnish were then applied. The patent leather for the dash and splash boards, and the shafts, was soaked before being hand sewn by Grace Randall while it was wet.

Finally, the brass fittings were screwed into position on the shafts. The Gig was then ready for Sarah Louise to drive under the scrutiny of the judges in the show ring.

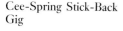

Cee-Spring Stick-Back Gig

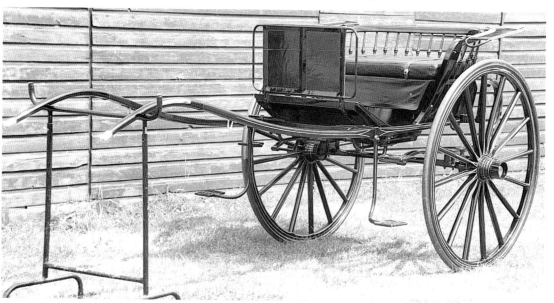

Pony Gig

PONY GIG

This Gig was designed and built by Mr Philip Holder of The Wellington Carriage Company in Shropshire, England, for Mrs Elizabeth Russell of Scotland. The design is based on the lines of an eighteenth-century Whisky. The body is framed in English ash. The panels are of birch plywood which is caned on the outer sides. The spares box folds out from beneath the seat which is upholstered in leather. Suspension is provided by leaf springs. The wheels are built traditionally using elm, oak and ash. They are fitted on modern taper roller bearings. Brass oil caps are used to complete the traditional appearance of this Gig.

235

Leftley Gig

LEFTLEY GIG

This Gig was designed and built by Mr and Mrs Reg Leftley, driving enthusiasts from Dyfed in Wales.

The traditionally styled body is moulded in glassfibre as are the splash and dash boards. The shafts are also made in glassfibre and are adjustable to accommodate animals of about one hand difference. The suspension is provided by semi-elliptic springs which are mounted on rubber bushes. The wheels are made of steel and run on sealed ball bearings. The wheel nuts are brass as are the shaft fittings and rein rail. The rubber tyres are held in clincher (also known as clencher) channels. All of the seating upholstery is detachable for ease of storage, cleaning and for keeping it away from the ravages of moths, and other undesirables, during the off season. This particular Leftley Gig is used regularly for showing by its owners, Col. and Mrs Barker-Simson of Braintree in Essex.

Show Cart

SHOW CART

The vehicle seen here was built in the U.S.A. by David L. Williams Company in Illinois. It is suitable for showing animals where the emphasis is on the horse or pony rather than the whole turnout. A great percentage of marks awarded in such classes in America are given for the animal and the way in which it performs. For this type of competition, it is essential to have a light vehicle from which the horse can be exhibited to full advantage in the same way that Show Wagons are used with hackneys. This Show Cart is light; the large wooden wheels enable it to be pulled easily and give the horse every opportunity to show extravagant action to catch the judge's eye.

The shafts, which bend down to either side of the axle, are plated with metal inside the curve. There is no dashboard so the reins go down to the driver's hands from the horse's quarters. Draught is taken through a swingletree and there are rat-tails to hold the crew holes of the traces onto the swingletree ends. Small straps around the swingletree and splinter bar restrict the play of the swingletree.

Norfolk Cart

NORFOLK CART

This Norfolk Cart was built by Croford Coachbuilders of Ashford in Kent, England. It is based on a traditional design and traditional materials were used in the construction. The mahogany body is built onto an ash frame. The shafts, which run outside the body, are of ash and steam-bent to shape. Suspension is provided by side, semi-elliptic springs. The rear step gives access to the rear-facing occasional seat which can accommodate two lightweight children. The wheels are of ash and elm, and they rotate on an original Collinge axle which came from Croford's store of traditional axles. The oil caps are also of the traditional design. The wheels are shod with clincher rubber tyres. This vehicle is finished in eight layers of modern paints.

HAREWOOD TWO-WHEELED DOG CART

This Dog Cart was built for the author by craftsmen at The Harewood Carriage Company, on the lines of a century-old Mills' Dog Cart.

The front seat has a lazy back for the passenger, and high rails at the side and rear of the driver's box seat. The whole seat can be slid forward on runners to adjust the balance when passengers, such as two light children, are carried on the rear-facing seat. This rear seat has side rails which fold down inside the body when the rear seat is not in use and the front seat is pushed back.

There is a swingletree which is fixed to the splinter bar by broad straps. The draught is transmitted down to either side of the axle by two leather-covered chains. There are also fixed trace hooks on each end of the splinter bar which can be used if preferred. The swingletree is easily removed by undoing a couple of shackles at the end of the chains by the axle.

Harewood Two-Wheeled Dog Cart

This rear view shows the large amount of luggage space under the seats. It also illustrates the excellent design of the wheels; stress is minimised at the axle by the angle in which the spokes go down to the felloes as the bearing surface comes onto the road.

TWO-WHEELED DOG CART

The Dog Cart seen here was built for Miss Anne Grahame Johnstone of Suffolk, by Mr Nick Wood of Fairbourne Carriages in Kent, England. Miss Grahame Johnstone took various ideas for her drawings from nineteenth-century dog carts which had particularly pleased her artistic eye. She put them together to form her ideal carriage for showing her Welsh cob.

Mr Wood drew up the plans from Anne's design, and made the vehicle. Mahogany and ash were used for the body, and the grains and colours of the woods are maintained through the ten or more layers of varnish in which the Dog Cart is finished. The back-to-back seating enables two lightweight children to be carried on the rear-facing seat; the front seat slides forward on runners to adjust the balance in that event. The design of the rear-seat cushion is unusual. It is made so that it folds in half along its length when the front seat is pushed back; when the front seat goes forward, the cushion is unfolded.

The shafts are made of laminated ash and have dees fitted to enable either full or false breeching to be used. The body is hung on side springs. The wooden wheels run on original Mail axles from Mr Wood's store of old axles.

Two-Wheeled Dog Cart

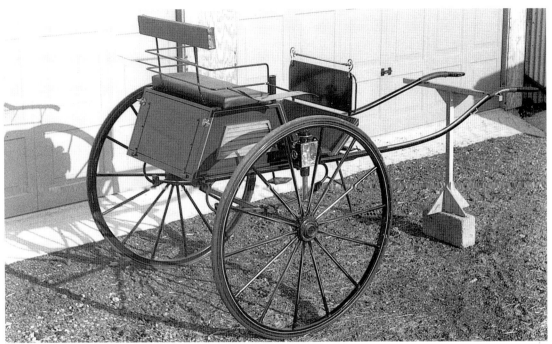

Crowland Dog Cart

CROWLAND DOG CART

This Dog Cart was built by Crowlands and belongs to Mrs Eunice Gleissberg of Suffolk, England.

It was constructed as a general purpose vehicle having two sets of shafts and a splinter bar which are easily interchangeable. Illustrated here, are the metal shafts, which are suitable for cross-country driving; these can be changed for the wooden shafts and splinter bar to give a more comfortable ride for showing or road driving. The vehicle is made of steel, apart from the decorative louvres which are made of wood.

ALFRISTON SPORTSMAN

The Alfriston Sportsman was designed and built by Mr Brian King of Alfriston Carriages in New Zealand.

The body of this general-purpose, competition Gig, is constructed of steel. The dash and splash boards, back rest, spares tray and seat are made of wood. The seat is adjustable to enable the vehicle to be balanced correctly. The spares tray, under the floor, has a hinged

Alfriston Sportsman

lid. The body is hung on Dennett springing with 'tie-down' straps to limit their travel when crossing rough terrain at speed in a Combined Driving Marathon. The wheels are made of steel and run on sealed ball bearings turning on a steel axle. They are held in place by bronze nuts. The tyres are moulded polyurethane and retained by welded flanges.

The vehicle, which is illustrated here, is used regularly by its builder for eventing and showing as well as for everyday driving.

Fenix Ralli Car

FENIX RALLI CAR

The Fenix Ralli Car is built by Mr Mark Broadbent of Fenix Enterprises in Devon, England, as a general-purpose vehicle to withstand the rigours of a cross-country course as well as being used for showing.

The vehicle has wooden panels on a steel framework. Laminated wood is used to give the traditional Ralli Car curve to the upper parts of the splash boards above the slatted sides of the body. The shafts, which are also of laminated wood, run through the inside of the body. The seat can be moved backwards and forwards as desired to obtain the required balance. The tail board lets down to give access to the large storage space under the seat. Suspension is provided by Dennett-type springing. The wheels of this Ralli Car are of the artillery design. Some Fenix Ralli Cars are built with traditional wooden wheels and box hubs.

JOHN WILLIE CART

This John Willie Cart was built for the author by the Serjeant family of Burley in Hampshire, England. The vehicle takes its name from the Serjeants' highly successful piebald driving pony, John Willie.

The plywood body is fitted onto a metal frame. The metal wheels rotate on sealed roller bearings. Each is held in place by four bolts

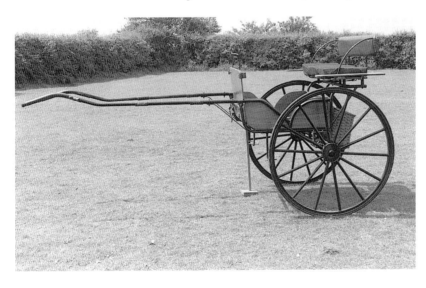

John Willie Cart

and can be taken off either by undoing the four nuts on the innerside of the hub, or by removing the centre nut on the axle. The tubular metal shafts can be taken off for travelling by removing four nuts and bolts. Suspension is provided by short, indispension units which give little relief on bumpy ground, but the cart does, however, give a very stable ride across country. Spares can be carried in the basket under the seat.

The vehicle was built to a specified weight of 90 kilos and a track width of 140 centimetres for competing with a pony at a driving trial in the 1980s.

BENNINGTON BACK-STEP BUGGY

The Bennington Back-Step Buggy is Mr and Mrs Michael Mart's best seller from their Artistic Iron Products workshops at Long Bennington in Nottinghamshire, England. Their daughter is a regular competitor in horse-driving trials.

This dual-purpose vehicle has a wide back step which can be taken off when it is not needed. The step is particularly useful when training young horses or when going across country because it affords a relatively safe place for the groom or passenger to travel. He or she is able to step off quickly to get to the animal's head if there is a problem. The presence of a person on the back step aids stability over rough terrain or round sharp turns when the driver may be competing against time. The passenger is able to stand on the step, holding onto the rear rails of the Buggy, whilst leaning out to keep the vehicle upright.

The body consists of a metal space frame of tubular steel, clad with specially selected, pretreated plywood. The balance of the Buggy is easily altered to suit the differing weights of the driver and passenger, and whether or not the back step is in use. The Bennington screw mechanism is operated with a handle at the rear of the vehicle which causes the body to run backwards and forwards along chromed steel slides, as the handle is turned.

The seat is padded and can be adjusted to suit the varying leg lengths of drivers. There is a spacious box for spares under the seat.

Suspension is on units, built by Bennington, which give adequate springing but not too much bounce.

The plastic-coated, tubular aluminium shafts are adjustable for height, length and width to accommodate different animals within a certain size range.

Brass fittings are used for the shafts, rein rail, wheel centres and spares box.

The wheels, which run on large taper roller bearings, are built by specialist craftsmen using the latest technology. They are fabricated from specially extruded aluminium with clincher channels to take the rubber tyres. Hoola hoops can be fitted, by means of wing nuts and bolts, to extend both wheels to the required width for cone courses at horse-driving trials.

Bennington Back-Step Buggy

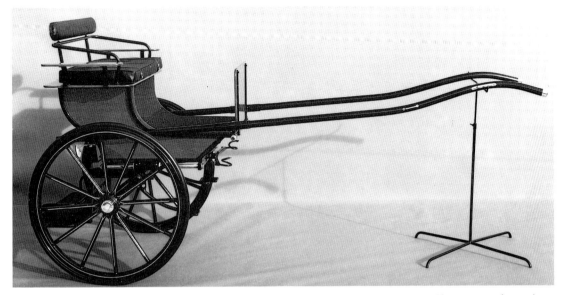

This picture shows the back step and the screw mechanism. A hoola hoop is fitted to the near-side wheel to enable comparison with the off-side wheel which does not have one fitted in this illustration. Of course, a vehicle would never be driven with just one hoola hoop.

245

GENESIS COMPETITION VEHICLE

Genesis Competition
Vehicle

The Genesis Competition Vehicle was designed and built by Mr
Philip Turner's Genesis Engineering of Nottinghamshire, England,
for all phases of a horse-driving trial.

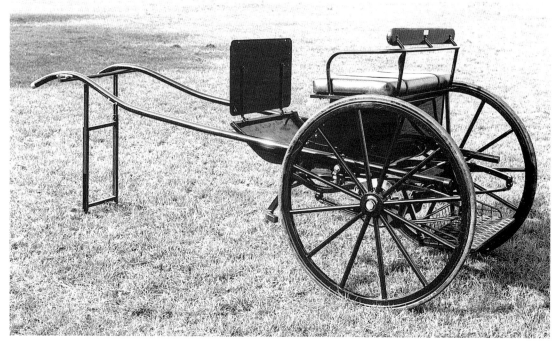

Unusual use is made of the principle of a cranked axle to alter the centre of gravity from high for the dressage and cones, to low for the marathon. No spanner or special tools are needed for this surprisingly quick adjustment. It is achieved by pulling out two pins, taking out and reversing the cranked ends of the axle and replacing the pins. When this is altered, the wheel track can also be changed to the width required to comply with competition rules.

The steel-framed body is clad with aluminium panels. It can be moved backwards and forwards, using the stainless steel mechanism and slides, to enable the vehicle to be balanced according to whether the groom is sitting alongside the driver or standing on the back step. This step can be removed if it is not needed. The seat is adjustable by means of a lever, to suit the length of the driver's legs. The mounting steps act as nudge bars to ward off posts or trees which might otherwise get caught between the wheel and the body.

Suspension is provided by semi-elliptic leaf springs with shock absorbers. The hydraulic disc brakes are foot operated. The wheels are made from fabricated steel with high tensile spokes. They run on high tensile axle stubs with taper roller bearings. The bolts which attach the shafts to the body frame are fitted with rubber bushes to allow some lateral movement. They can be altered for length, height and width within certain limits.

The overall weight is approximately 145 kilos, leaving a margin of 5 kilos to include spares. The vehicle has a brass rein rail and is finished in numerous layers of paint. One of these vehicles is driven in competitions by the designer's wife.

OPPOSITE
Above: The Genesis Competition Vehicle on the higher axle setting with all brasswork and lamps ready for presentation and dressage.
Below: The same Genesis Competition Vehicle on the lower setting for marathon work, with the brass, lamps and mudguards taken off and the back step fitted.

WITHYBROOK CHARIOT

Mr Rodney Ousbey of Withybrook Carriages, Warwickshire, England, first competed in driving trials with a nineteenth-century Governess Cart to which he added a back step for his groom. Realising that a century-old vehicle would not continue to stand up to the rigours of the marathon, he decided to design and build a vehicle he could use for such competitions incorporating some of the traditional features of the Governess Cart; the Withybrook Chariot was the result.

The low-slung body is hung between full-elliptic springs giving good suspension and the low centre of gravity for which the Governess Cart was renowned. Clincher rubber-shod, metal wheels are hung on the axle which runs through the buck. The draught is taken on the axle, from the swingletree, via padded chains which are retained at the desired height by rings on each side of the front of the body. The low back-step gives easy mounting and access.

This design has since been copied by builders in the U.S.A. A similar version of this vehicle is becoming known as a 'Withybrook'. Perhaps this is also because it resembles, in many ways, the American Meadowbrook Cart.

Withybrook Chariot

FENIX COMPETITION GIG

This Gig is built by Mr Mark Broadbent of Fenix Enterprises in Devon, England. It was designed for use with ponies, both for marathon driving and for everyday activities.

The steel-framed body is built onto an axle which telescopes so that the width of the wheels can be adjusted as required for the

Fenix Competition Gig

248

marathon and cone phases of a driving trial. Artillery-type wheels are used. A groom's bolt-on standing platform can be fitted for marathon driving. There is a sliding body system so the whole balance and weight distribution can be altered.

ALFRISTON MINI

This little vehicle was designed and built by Mr Brian King of Alfriston Carriages in the North Island of New Zealand specifically for use with small ponies and donkeys. The lightweight construction makes it particularly popular with donkey owners and has enabled a number of these enthusiasts to discover and enjoy the sport of driving.

The low-slung body is framed with tubular steel and hung on quarter-elliptic springs. A swingletree is fitted enabling a breast collar to be used. The Mini shown here has moulded plastic wheels with pneumatic tyres. A de luxe Mini is produced with Alfriston steel or aluminium wheels.

Alfriston Mini

DARENT CARRIAGE

Interest in driving for disabled drivers, through The Riding for the Disabled Association, has grown considerably during the past decade. There are numerous approved Driving Groups within the officially recognised regions throughout the country. Weekly driving sessions are held by a lot of Group organisers, involving a great many able-bodied and disabled drivers. This has resulted in increased demand for suitable vehicles which are built specially to carry both ambulant disabled drivers and those in wheelchairs. As drivers have gained confidence, so showing classes and performance events have been organised specifically for these enthusiasts in their specially-constructed carriages.

Ken Jackson Carriages have specialised in making suitable vehicles including the Darent Carriage illustrated here. It is suitable for a small pony, having wire wheels with heavy duty pneumatic tyres. Metal carriage wheels, with clincher rubber tyres, can be fitted to enable the vehicle to be used with a larger pony. The shafts can be adjusted to cater for animals between 10.2 h.h. and 13.2 h.h. The well-padded seats slide on runners to obtain the correct balance, and they are also removable so that, if a wheelchair is carried, one of the seats can be taken out.

Above: Darent Carriage showing folding ramp
Below: Darent Carriage

The wheelchair and occupant are wheeled into the cart up the integral folding ramp. This has spring-loaded, anti-rattle catches. The wheelchair can be held in place by adjustable chocks or by ambulance-type wheelchair clamps. If carriage-type wheels are used to accommodate a larger pony, then longer loading ramps are fitted to suit the higher floor thus avoiding too steep a slope. If the driver is ambulant, the off-side seat remains in place. Large, rubber-covered mounting steps afford easier access for such a driver than the smaller traditional type of gig steps.

Suspension is provided by leaf springs. The wooden parts of the Darent are stained and varnished to give a smart appearance. The weight is about 110 kilos.

DOUBLE-SEATED SLEIGH

This Sleigh was built in the U.S.A., by David Williams Company of Illinois, to accommodate four people. The seats are similar in design to that which is used on the Single-Seat Buggy being fully padded and upholstered for warmth and comfort.

Weather conditions are frequently ideal for sleighing in many parts of the U.S.A. when enthusiasts get together for driving rallies in the snow.

Double-Seated Sleigh

WAGONETTE

The Wagonette shown overleaf was built by J. A. Jacks & Sons of Hay-on-Wye, Wales, and was numbered 72.

The metal body accommodates the driver and one passenger on the forward-facing front seat, and two adults or four children on the inward-facing rear seats. Access to the rear is simple and safe as there is a large, low, rear mounting-step and wide mounting-handles.

Wagonette

Full lock enables the pair of ponies to be turned at right angles to the body which is essential for negotiating hazards at a horse trial or turning in narrow places when driving around the lanes.

The brake blocks can be applied to the rear wheels by either the handbrake or the foot brake. Roller bolts are fitted to the moveable swingletrees on the splinter bar so that breast collars can be employed, if required, using traces with traditional quick-release ends. The brass hub caps can be put on for smart occasions. They can be replaced with black metal caps when the vehicle is used for cross-country activities. The lining on the wheels and springs is achieved with stick-on striping, as used on some motorcar bodies. This vehicle is in the author's collection.

The Wagonette from the rear showing full lock

ALFRISTON COUNTRYMAN

The Alfriston Countryman was designed as an all-purpose vehicle. It was built by its designer, Mr Brian King, of Alfriston Carriages in New Zealand's North Island. The version shown here takes its form from the style of the wagonette, but the positions of the rear seats can be interchanged, as needed, for varying requirements.

The structural components are of steel and the panels are made of wood. The body is hung on four full-elliptic springs which give a firm but comfortable ride both with a light load and when six adults are carried. The steel wheels run on sealed ball bearings which turn on a steel axle. They are retained by bronze nuts. The external contracting brakes are foot operated and act on the rear wheel hubs via a cable.

There is a drawer for spares under the rear platform. The large rear step gives easy access for grooms. A hinged pole and swingletree assembly, with limited travel, can be fitted when the vehicle is used with a pair, as can a swingletree and shaft assembly to accommodate a single pony in a breast collar.

This vehicle was used by its builder in Combined Driving Events in New Zealand throughout 1989 and 1990.

Alfriston Countryman

FENIX CHAMPION MARATHON VEHICLE

This vehicle has been designed and developed by Mr Mark Broadbent of Fenix Enterprises in Devon, England, for use in the marathon phase of horse-driving trials.

The body is constructed with a steel frame onto which the panels are bolted. The driver's seat is fully adjustable and has a built-in anti-shock system. The rear platform has a guard to prevent a groom's foot from slipping into a wheel. There are solid grab handles to facilitate easy mounting and make it safer when travelling over rough terrain, or if, when cornering at speed, grooms 'hang out' to help their driver. Rear seats can be fitted if required.

The rear suspension consists of low-pivot independent swinging arms, controlled by coil-spring gas damper units. The front suspension consists of leaf springs on a solid, high tensile, steel axle. The spring rate and ride height are adjustable. The wheels, which are of the artillery type, run on taper roller bearings and are close coupled. Disc brakes are fitted to the rear wheels. Front-wheel brakes can be fitted if required and engineered to work either simultaneously or independently as needed. Both are foot operated. The handbrake is used for parking. The pole height is adjustable and has fully sprung and dampened support. It is also designed to enable quick release if necessary. The swingletree ends are protected by a fender to help to shield the trace end if a hazard is hit.

The vehicle is made to standard F.E.I. weight and width.

A carriage of this type was driven by its builder for several seasons with a pony team in driving trials.

Fenix Champion
Marathon Vehicle

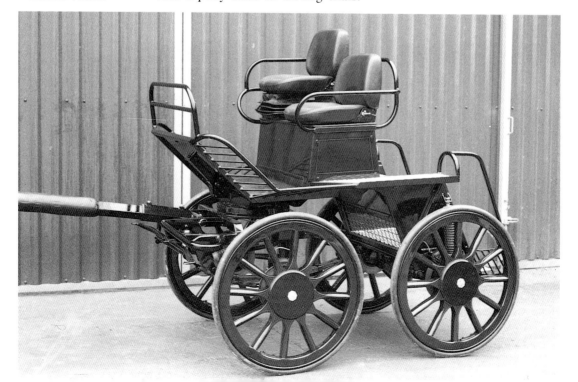

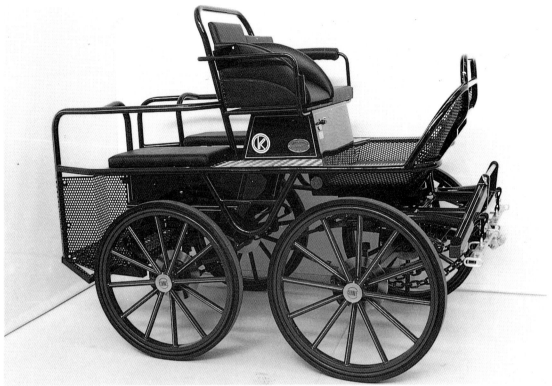

KÜHNLE MARATHON CARRIAGE

Kühnle Marathon
Carriage

This marathon vehicle was built by Paul and Gustav Kühnle's carriage manufacturers' in West Germany. The vehicle is commonly known, amongst horse-trials drivers throughout the world, as a 'Kühnle'. It is built to weights and widths to comply with International rules and has numerous features which are required by competitors.

The driver's seat is sprung and shaped to hold the Whip in place over rough terrain, and padded to prevent bruising. The rear accommodation is built to enable grooms to sit or stand as desired. Independent front and rear disc brakes are fitted to the metal wheels. The rubber tyres are wider than usual to prevent them from sinking as deeply into mud or sand as tyres of the traditional width. The lower parts of the body are panelled with mesh to allow water to flow freely when a water hazard is being negotiated. There is structure between the front and rear wheels to ward off trees or posts which might otherwise cause the vehicle to become jammed. The steel pole is adjustable for length; it is sprung to prevent jarring and strain on the front axle. Quick release shackles enable traces to be freed instantly should the need arise.

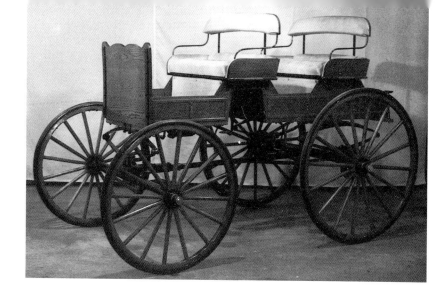

Bronson Wagon

BRONSON WAGON

This Bronson Wagon was built in Illinois, U.S.A., by David L. Williams Company to a traditional design.

The Siamese Phaeton-type seating accommodates the driver and three passengers. There is space for luggage behind and below the rear seat. The varnished oak body is built on a perch undercarriage with one transverse full-elliptic spring at the front and two longitudinal full-elliptic springs at the rear. The arch in the body enables the hickory wheels to turn, giving a half lock, until they contact the roller bar on the perch.

The Wagon can be fitted with shafts to take a single horse or with a pole for a pair. Because the pole is made complete with splinter bar and swingletrees to fit into a flexible attachment on the front axle, it is necessary for a yoke to be used with the harness in order that the end of the pole is held up by the horses through their collars.

FOUR-WHEELED DOG CART

This Dog Cart was built, using a traditional design, by Mr Nick Wood of Fairbourne Carriages in Kent, England. The body is made from ash and mahogany, and seats four people. The tail board lets down to form a foot rest for the rear-facing passengers. The wooden wheels run on Collinge axles taken from Mr Wood's store of original axles. Traditional brake blocks are used on the rear wheels which are brought into action by a handbrake. The wheels are shod with clincher rubber tyres.

Four-Wheeled Dog Cart
(Fairbourne)

FOUR-WHEELED DOG CART

This traditionally designed Dog Cart was built by Croford Coach-builders of Ashford in Kent, England. Traditional materials were used in the construction. The mahogany body, was built on an ash frame. The louvres, under the rear seat, give ventilation to any dogs which may be carried. Suspension is provided by four full-elliptic springs. The wheels are made of ash and elm; they rotate on original Collinge axles which came from Croford's store. They are shod with rubber in clincher channels. The Dog Cart is finished with several coats of modern varnish which shows the grain of the woods. It has shafts for use with a single animal, and a splinter bar and pole can be fitted to take a pair, unicorn or team.

Four-Wheeled Dog Cart
(Croford's)

257

Fenix High-Seat
Sporting Dog Cart

FENIX HIGH-SEAT SPORTING
DOG CART

This High-Seat Sporting Dog Cart is built by Mr Mark Broadbent of Fenix Enterprises in Devon, England. It combines a traditional appearance (apart from the disc brakes which are optional) with modern constructional techniques.

This carriage is as suitable for showing with a pair, unicorn or team, as it is for the presentation and dressage phases of a horse-driving trial. The high seat puts the driver into a position on the box, which gives a very 'coaching' flavour.

258

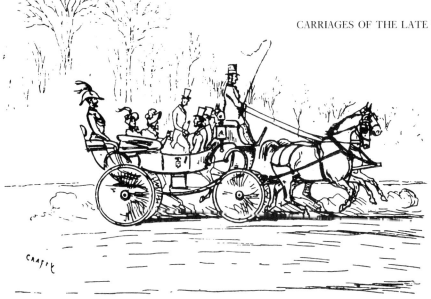

CAVALIER'S BREAK

This Cavalier's Break was built to a traditional English design by the Kühnle Carriage Manufacturers in West Germany. A total of eight people can be accommodated. The luxurious buttoned-leather, vis-à-vis seating in the body is similar to that of a Sociable. Two steps facilitate entry and the doors keep dirt and draughts from the four occupants. The driver is accommodated on a high wedge-shaped box seat above a louvred boot. He can operate the disc

Cavalier's Break

brakes with his foot and the rear-wheel brake blocks with a pull-on handbrake. The front-seat passenger has a lower cushion beside the Whip. Two grooms can travel on the high rear seats from which they can watch the horses over the heads of the passengers. Spare bars are carried below the groom's seat and a spare, jointed, whip on a board, is fastened to the framework of the lazy back. There is a hind boot under the groom's feet for spares and other items. The wheels are made of wood and rotate on roller bearings. Draught is taken from the traces onto roller bolts on the splinter bar.

ROOF-SEAT BREAK

This Break, which is now in Italy, was designed and built by Mr Nick Wood of Fairbourne Carriages in Kent, England. He examined and took measurements from several original Breaks in order to draw his working plans. Mr Wood's main objective was that the result of his research should be 'pleasing to the eye'.

This Roof-Seat Break has a distinctly 'coaching' flavour; the driver's box seat is similar to that on a coach. The rear seats are supported on iron stays. The centre seat accommodates a further three passengers.

Mahogany, ash and modern materials were used in the construction. There is boot space under the front seat. The hind boot is fitted with a picnic tray and cellaret, and is similar in many ways to that on a Private Drag. Suspension is provided by four full-elliptic springs. The wooden wheels are iron shod; they run on original Collinge axles which are finished to give an exterior appearance of Mail axles. The vehicle can be drawn by a pair, unicorn or team.

Roof-Seat Break

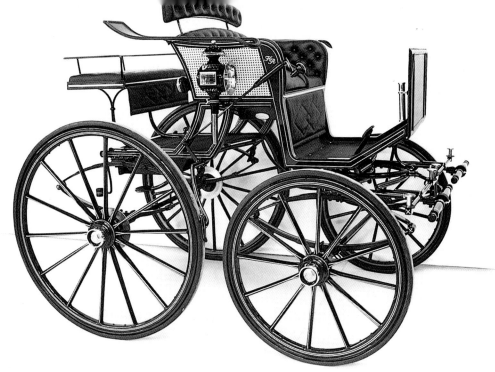

Spider Phaeton

SPIDER PHAETON

The Spider Phaeton illustrated here was built in West Germany to an original English design by Kühnle Carriage Manufacturers. It is suitable for the dressage phase of a horse-driving trial or for showing in private driving and Concours d'Elegance classes.

The seating is upholstered in buttoned leather and there is a wedge-shaped box for the driver. The outer sides of the body are covered in cane to give a light and elegant appearance. The padded rear seat accommodates the groom and has a valance to keep draughts off the backs of his legs. There is a box for spares under the floor below the groom's feet which is opened from the rear. The splash and dash boards are leather covered.

Suspension is provided by four full-elliptic springs. The disc brakes are foot operated and there is a wind-on handbrake which applies blocks to the rear wheels for parking. The wheels are of wood. The axles have roller bearings. The Phaeton has both swingletrees and roller bolts on a splinter bar, enabling the horses to be driven in either breast or full collars.

DEMI-MAIL PHAETON

The Demi-Mail Phaeton seen overleaf was built to a traditional design by Mr John Gapp of Norfolk, England, for Mr John Parker and

261

Miss Susan Townsend, also of Norfolk. This carriage enables Susan to show her Connemara ponies to full advantage.

The leather hood can be raised, as in the photograph, to give protection from bad weather, or lowered on a fine day. The body of the Phaeton was built with mahogany on an ash frame. The dash and splash boards are covered with patent leather to match that on the harness which Susan makes for all the animals she and John drive. The suspension is provided by full-elliptic springs in front, and telegraph springs at the rear. The brake blocks, which act on iron tyres on the wooden wheels, can be either foot or hand operated. The handbrake lever lies between the driver's cushion and the inside of the hood. The metal round the hubs of the front wheels has flats for use as mounting steps by the driver and passenger. There are two steps which give access to the rear seat enabling the grooms to mount in unison if two are being carried because a four-in-hand is being shown.

Grooms who practise this correctly can add greatly to the presentation of a team in the show ring. As the Whip nods to the grooms

Demi-Mail Phaeton

to stand aside, and the team is given the office to walk forward, the groom who was at the leaders' heads steps to one side and walks smartly towards the rear of the carriage. The other groom, who was at the wheelers' heads on the other side, turns, pauses, then walks in step with the first groom so that both reach their mounting step at the same time. They both place a foot on their step and a hand on their mounting handle, as the carriage passes, and reach their seats to sit down exactly together. It is impressive when perfection in this seemingly small act is achieved by two immaculately turned-out grooms.

SINGLE-SEATED BUGGY

The Buggy illustrated here was built in Illinois, U.S.A., by David L. Williams Company. It is constructed to a traditional American design with a wooden body and leather dash board. The driver and one passenger are carried in comfort in the fully padded, upholstered seat. There is boot space behind the seat. The undercarriage is made with a perch and two transverse full-elliptic springs. The shape of the buck restricts the turning lock to 45 degrees because the wheels contact the rollers on the sides of the body once a quarter lock is reached.

This Buggy is so light that it is quite easy to lift the back end by the rear axle and move it sideways, should the vehicle have to be turned in a restricted area.

Mounting can be difficult as it is necessary to climb between the wheels, to reach the mounting step. Often, horses are trained to step across to one side, without moving forward, to allow the driver to mount and then to step across to the other side to allow the passenger to mount. In both America and Australia, where vehicles of this design are common, it is quite usual to see an apparently spirited horse well trained enough to perform this manoeuvre without any fuss or difficulty.

Single-Seated Buggy

263

MONTFORT VICTORIA

This Victoria was built by Mick and Rosemary Saunders' Company, Montfort Carriage Builders of Herefordshire.

The demand for horse-drawn wedding carriages has increased during the past few years, and the Victoria is an ideal carriage for transporting a bride to and from the Church. The low mounting step affords easy access to the rear, forward-facing, seat. When the small door is shut, protection is given to the dress from dirt thrown up from the wheels. The leather cloth hood can be raised, as shown here, to give protection from rain, or lowered if the weather is fine. There is an occasional seat behind and below the coachman's seat, which can be unfolded to accommodate two more passengers such as bridesmaids or pages. The Victoria is driven by a coachman who is accompanied by a groom on the high, forward-facing, seat under which there is a spares box.

The hydraulic drum brakes operate on the rear axle from the coachman's foot pedal. Suspension is provided, at the rear, by threequarter-elliptic springs as this arrangement does not allow the back axle to be forced backwards when the brake is applied. Full-elliptic springs are fitted at the front. The wheel arch permits full lock for maximum manoeuvrability. The vehicle is built on a steel chassis and clad with marine plywood. The dash and splash boards on this particular vehicle are made of wood, but some Montfort Victorias have leather-covered splash and dash boards.

The vehicle can be fitted with a pole for a pair, or shafts for a single horse.

Montfort Victoria

VIS-À-VIS

This Vis-à-Vis was built by David L. Williams Company in Illinois, U.S.A. Six passengers can be carried on the face-to-face seats inside, which can be protected from sun or rain by the hood.

Brakes to the rear wheels are foot operated by the driver. The wheels are made of hickory. Suspension is provided by three full-elliptic springs to give a very comfortable ride. The double perch undercarriage restricts the turning lock to less than a half. The vehicle can be drawn by a single horse or a pair.

Vis-à Vis

Landau

LANDAU

The Landau shown here was built by Kühnle Carriage Manufacturers in Beihingen, West Germany, for the Sultan of Oman.

The body of the carriage takes the form of a Sefton Landau, having a canoe-shaped outline. Four people are accommodated on the viv-à-vis seating. The Landau can be used as a closed carriage, as seen here, with the hoods raised, or as an open vehicle with the hoods folded down. When the hoods are lowered, the side windows slide down into the frames of the doors.

The disc brakes are foot operated by the coachman. There is also a wind-on brake which is hand operated to bring the brake blocks against the fronts of the rear wheels for parking. The rubber-shod, wooden wheels rotate on roller bearings. Swingletrees are fitted enabling the pair to be driven in breast collars if desired.

CONCORD STAGECOACH
(Abbot and Downing, Western Style)

Mr Homer Easterwood of Texas, U.S.A., is the instigator of Recreated Originals. He and his staff use the same techniques and specialised equipment the original craftsmen used over a century ago. He constructs coaches which are exact replicas of the 'Western-Style Abbot and Downing Concord Stagecoaches'.

The quality of the timber is considered to be so important that the wood has to be transported about 2,000 miles across the United States of America in order to obtain the best available grades of hickory, ash, oak, elm and poplar. Leather for the interior and items such as the cushions and the luggage trunks is brought from Oregon where it is cured and prepared by the old methods.

The iron work is forged on site in the blacksmith's shop. Decorative painting on the bright red body, and striping on the 'straw yellow' wheels and gear, is carried out by a specialist striper. Trimming for the nine-seat interior to the Coach is done by outworkers.

Concord Stagecoach
(Abbot and Downing,
Western Style)

Above: Detail of interior
of the 'Eastern-Style
Abbot and Downing
Stagecoach' showing the
strong padded, lazy-back,
strap against which
passengers who are
seated on the central
bench (not shown) could
lean during their journey.
Below: 'Eastern-Style
Stagecoach' detail
showing the roof seating.
Also seen here are the
leather flap window
coverings.

Concord Stagecoach
(Abbot and Downing,
Eastern Style)

The pole and swing poles are reinforced with iron, as they were
on the original Coaches, enabling two, four, six or eight horses to be
hitched and driven from the front seat.

The weight of the Coach is about 909 kilos.

CONCORD STAGECOACH
(Abbot and Downing, Eastern Style)

This is another American Stagecoach which has been built in
Mr Homer Easterwood's Recreated Originals workshops, by his
dedicated craftsmen.

The design differs from the 'Western-Style Abbot and Downing
Stagecoach', as can be seen by comparing the illustrations of both
Coaches. This Coach is built to accommodate numerous 'outside'
passengers on the roof and on the dickey seat, as well as the nine
'inside' travellers.

STATE COACH

The State Coach seen here was constructed, and is owned, by Mr Philip Holder of The Wellington Carriage Company in Shropshire, England. It was completed in 1982 having been built over a period of three years as an exercise in traditional coach building. The plans for the Coach were based on details taken from a number of existing vehicles of this type as it was not possible to obtain a complete set of original working drawings.

The body and undercarriage are made of ash, and the panels are of birch ply. There is a considerable amount of hand carving and moulded work. Most of the ironwork was fabricated using ark welding but it has been carefully finished to render it indistinguishable from forged work. The Coach is fitted with cee and under springs, and the body is suspended on leather braces. The interior is trimmed with blue cloth and twenty metres of wool trimming were used in the hammer cloth. Folding steps are concealed behind the doors.

State Coach

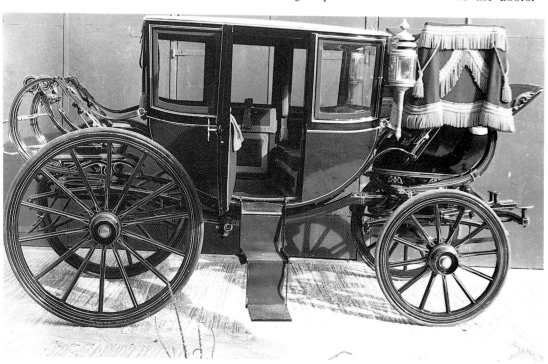

Australian State Coach

AUSTRALIAN STATE COACH

The Australian State Coach was built in New South Wales by a team of craftsmen who were directed by Mr J. Frecklington. The Coach was presented to Her Majesty The Queen, in Canberra, in May 1988 as a gift from the people in Australia's bicentennial year. It was first used in November 1988 by The Queen and The Duke of Edinburgh when travelling to the State Opening of Parliament.

The frame of the Australian State Coach is made of mild steel. The black body is made of steel and sixteen-gauge aluminium, and is hung on cee springs. The perch is made of Australian spotted-gum timber which is laminated, to obtain the desired curves, and plated for strength. The wheels are made of mountain ash for the felloes, spotted gum for the spokes and iron bark for the hubs. They are painted in signal red and lined with gold. The rubber tyres are held into the metal channels by two wires which run through the rubber, round the wheel. Red-cedar timber was used for the interior of the Coach which was bordered with a trim of book-matched elm burr veneer.

Twenty-nine metres of blue silk brocade, supplied by The Royal Mews department at Buckingham Palace, were used for the upholstery. The crystal in the interior is Waterford Crystal, as are the lamps. The interior lighting, heating and windows are electrically operated; the battery unit providing the power is within the footman's seat. This Royal Claret seat has The Queen's Commonwealth Insignia painted on either side with The Coat of Arms of Australia in gold-plated casting on the back. The footman operates the brake from his seat because the Coach is drawn by four or six horses with two or three postillions.

The Queen's heraldic artist, Mr Geoffrey Francis, flew to Australia to carry out the specialised work of the heraldic painting on the Coach.

The roof of the Coach is lavishly decorated with ornamentation and finished in gold leaf.

This is the first new State Coach to come into The Royal Mews Collection since 1910.

Index